ICELAND TRAVEL GUIDE 2024

Your Up-To-Date Comprehensive Companion for
Exploring Iceland's Cities and Landscapes with
Practical Tips, Cultural Insights, and Detailed
Itineraries

Katrin Frost

Katrín Frost

Contents

DISCALIMER

Nature of Content:

The content within this travel guide is intended to provide a general overview of various attractions, accommodations, and cultural elements in Iceland. It may contain generalizations and repetitive information that are necessary for comprehensive coverage. The descriptions and advice are formulated to serve broad audience needs and might not account for all individual preferences or specifics.

Source of Content:

This guide has been compiled using a combination professional traveler, artificial intelligence and publicly available data. While this content is uniqe, whe have the 100% of copyright & every effort has been made to ensure accuracy, the generated content may not capture the nuanced insights a human expert might offer.

Purpose of the Guide:

This guide is designed as an introductory resource for travelers planning to visit Iceland. It should be used as a starting point for trip planning and not as the sole source of all travel decisions. Readers are encouraged to seek additional, up-to-date information and verify any details critical to their travel plans.

Limitation of Liability:

While efforts have been made to provide valuable and accurate information, we do not assume any legal liability or responsibility for the accuracy, completeness, or usefulness of any information, product, or process disclosed herein. We do not guarantee that the information matches the current conditions, and usage of this guide is at the sole risk of the reader.

Informational Purpose:

This guide is provided for informational purposes only. It is not intended as a comprehensive or definitive guide to Iceland but as an aid to help facilitate travel planning.

Encouragement to Verify:

Due to the dynamic nature of travel information and the limitations of AI-generated content, we strongly advise travelers to verify travel conditions, local regulations, and safety measures with local authorities, service providers, and official resources before making travel arrangements.

By adhering to this disclaimer, users of the "Iceland Travel Guide 2024" can set appropriate expectations and use the guide most effectively, reducing the likelihood of dissatisfaction stemming from misconceptions about the guide's purpose and contents.

Heads Up About the Pictures in Your Book!

You might notice the pictures in your Iceland Guide are not in color. We kept them simple – black and white – so the book is easy to carry and read.

But guess what? We've got a cool bonus for you! When you get this book, you also get a FREE colorful eBook version. It's got all the awesome colors of Iceland's places, from blue icebergs to green northern lights!

Plus, you'll get some handy digital maps for your phone or tablet. These are super useful when you're out and about in Iceland.

At the end of your book, there's a simple way to get your colorful eBook and maps. We hope these goodies make getting ready for your Iceland trip even more fun!

Introduction

Welcome to Iceland, a place of incredible beauty and thrilling contrasts. Imagine standing under a sky glowing with Northern Lights or watching huge geysers shoot up into the air. Iceland isn't just a place to visit; it's a whole experience, a dance with nature's raw power.

You can find a lot of information about Iceland online for free, but nothing beats the insights from someone who actually lives there. This book is your starting guide, packed with everything you need to know from amazing spots and deep history to cool traditions and tasty food.

This guide is written to help you get the basics right and avoid common mistakes. It pulls together tips and info from people who've traveled across Iceland, so you can have a great trip without the usual travel hiccups. Remember, this book is just the beginning. The real magic of traveling comes from your own adventures and the surprises you find along the way.

We're here to help you get ready for your trip with all the must-know details about Iceland. Keep your mind open, stay curious, and let Iceland's adventurous spirit guide you through this stunning country. Enjoy your journey!

Chapter 1

Welcome to Iceland

INTRODUCTION TO ICELAND

Iceland is a land of contrasts, and not just because of its misleading name. Yes, there is ice, plenty of it in the form of majestic glaciers that would make a snow cone vendor weep with joy. But there is also fire. Not the kind that necessitates a call to your local fire department, but the kind that comes from the belly of the Earth itself, in the form of volcanoes and geysers. It's a country where you can soak in geothermal hot springs while watching the Northern Lights dance overhead. If that doesn't tickle your wanderlust, I don't know what will.

Now, the Icelanders themselves are a hearty bunch. You'd have to be to live in a place that experiences midnight sun in summer and near total darkness in winter. But don't let the extreme weather fool you. Icelanders are some of the most welcoming folks you'll ever meet. They have a knack for storytelling, a love for their unique language (which, incidentally, hasn't changed much since the Viking Age), and a deep respect for their environment.

Speaking of the environment, Iceland is a paradise for nature lovers. There are waterfalls that make Niagara look like a leaky faucet, mountains that make the Rockies look like molehills, and black sand beaches that...well, they're just black sand beaches, and they're utterly stunning. The wildlife, too, is something to behold. From puffins that look like they've flown straight out of a cartoon, to majestic whales that dwarf the boats observing them, Iceland is a veritable Eden of flora and fauna.

Then there's the food. Oh, the food! If you've never had the pleasure of tasting

Welcome to Iceland

Icelandic cuisine, you're in for a treat. From the freshest of fish to the most succulent lamb, Icelandic dishes are a testament to the country's abundant natural resources. And don't even get me started on the skyr, a type of Icelandic yogurt that's as thick as Greek yogurt but much milder in flavor. You haven't lived until you've had a bowl of skyr with a drizzle of Icelandic honey.

Quick Facts

Well, well, well, if it isn't the curious wanderer, ready to dive into the icy depths of quick facts about Iceland! Now, don't you fret, I ain't gonna bamboozle you with fancy words and highfalutin phrases. No siree, we're gonna keep things simple, just like how Icelanders like their hot dogs (with everything on it, by the way).

Now, let's start with a fun one, shall we? Did you know that this North Atlantic island is home to more sheep than humans? Yes, sir! The sheep population outnumbers the human population, making it the only country where the sheep can stage a successful coup if they ever develop political ambitions.

Iceland is not just about sheep, though. It's a land of fire and ice, quite literally. The country has about 130 volcanoes, some active, some not. But don't worry, the locals aren't living in constant fear of a volcanic eruption. In fact, they've harnessed the geothermal energy to heat their homes. Talk about turning a potential disaster into an advantage, eh?

Speaking of heating homes, Iceland's capital, Reykjavik, is the world's northernmost capital. It's also one of the cleanest, greenest, and safest cities in the world. And while we're on the topic of records, let's not forget that Iceland was one of the last places on earth to be settled by humans. It's like they saved the best for last!

We can't talk about Iceland without mentioning its stunning natural beauty. From geysers and waterfalls to glaciers and black sand beaches, it is a photographer's dream come true. And let's not forget the Northern Lights, nature's very own light show. These celestial lights, also known as Aurora Borealis, can be seen from September to April. Now, ain't that worth braving the cold?

Now, here's something that might tickle your funny bone. In Iceland, there are no surnames or family names. That's right, folks! They use the old Nordic naming system where a person's last name indicates the first name of their father or mother. So, if your name is John, and your father's name is Peter, you would be John Petersson. And if you're a girl, you'd be John Petersdottir. Quite a mouthful, ain't it?

And before you ask, yes, the phone book is listed by first names. Can you imagine trying to find a 'John' in an Icelandic phone book? You'd have better luck finding a needle in a haystack!

But don't let that deter you. Icelanders are some of the friendliest folks you'll ever meet. They all speak English, which is a relief because Icelandic is quite a tongue-twister. They also love their literature and have more writers per capita than any other country. Maybe the long, dark winters are good for something after all!

Now, let's talk about food, or more specifically, the lack thereof. Iceland is not known for its cuisine and for good reason. Traditional dishes include fermented shark and sheep's head. But don't worry, you'll also find more palatable options like seafood and lamb. And let's not forget the hot dogs. Icelanders love their hot dogs!

Quick Facts

- **Capital:** Reykjavik
- **Currency:** Icelandic Króna (ISK)
- **Language:** Icelandic; English widely spoken
- **Best Travel Months:** June to August for mild weather; October to March for Northern Lights
- **Driving:** Right-hand side; International Driving Permit required for non-EU licenses
- **Electricity:** 230 V, 50 Hz, plug types C and F
- **Emergency Numbers:** General emergency - 112
- **Tipping Etiquette:** Not customary; service charges included in most bills
- **Water Safety:** Tap water is safe and drinkable throughout Iceland
- **Internet Access:** Widely available; high-speed connections common in urban areas, slower in remote regions
- **Population:** Approximately 360,000
- **Time Zone:** GMT (Greenwich Mean Time) year-round
- **Climate:** Subarctic maritime; cool summers and mild winters
- **National Day:** June 17, celebrating independence from Denmark in 1944
- **Popular Dishes:** Hákarl (fermented shark), Plokkfiskur (fish stew), Skyr (Icelandic yogurt)
- **Unique Wildlife:** Puffins, Icelandic horses, Arctic foxes
- **Public Transport:** Reliable bus service in Reykjavik; limited services in rural areas
- **Visa Requirements:** Part of the Schengen Area; visa-free for many countries for up to 90 days
- **Hiking Seasons:** Best from June to September; weather-dependent
- **Famous Festivals:** Iceland Airwaves (music), Reykjavik Pride, and the Secret Solstice Festival
- **Typical Souvenirs:** Lopapeysa (woolen sweaters), volcanic rock jewelry, Icelandic literature

Welcome to Iceland

- **Shopping Hours:** Typically 10 AM to 6 PM on weekdays, shorter on weekends
- **Alcohol Purchase:** Sold at licensed venues and state-operated Vínbúðin stores; high taxes on alcohol
- **Smoking Laws:** Banned in bars, restaurants, and public spaces
- **Average Temperature:** Varies from -1°C in winter to 14°C in summer
- **Main Airports:** Keflavík International Airport (near Reykjavik), Akureyri Airport in the north
- **Local Cuisine:** Dominated by seafood, lamb, and dairy products
- **ATM Availability:** Common in cities and towns, scarcer in remote areas
- **Camping Regulations:** Strict; camping allowed only in designated areas
- **Natural Attractions:** Geysers, glaciers, volcanic landscapes, and thermal hot springs

Map Of Iceland

Location and Appeal of Iceland

Iceland, often described as the "Land of Fire and Ice," is situated in the North Atlantic Ocean, strategically located between Europe and North America. This island nation lies just below the Arctic Circle, with Greenland to its west and Norway and the British Isles to its east. Its precise coordinates are approximately 65 degrees north latitude and 18 degrees west longitude.

Reasons to Visit Iceland:

- **Spectacular Landscapes:**
- Iceland's natural beauty is unparalleled, featuring an array of landscapes that captivate visitors. From the explosive power of geysers and the tranquil beauty of its numerous waterfalls, such as Gullfoss and Skógafoss, to the eerie calm of its vast lava fields and the majestic presence of its glaciers like Vatnajökull, Iceland offers a natural spectacle unlike any other.
- **Unique Geological Features:**
- As a hotspot of volcanic and geothermal activity, Iceland provides unique opportunities to explore phenomena such as active volcanoes, soothing hot springs, and expansive geothermal fields. The Blue Lagoon, a geothermal spa, is one of many such places where visitors can experience the therapeutic properties of geothermally heated waters.
- **Cultural Richness:**

- Beyond its environmental allure, Iceland is steeped in rich history and culture, dating back to its settlement by Norse Vikings in the 9th century. Reykjavik, the capital, along with being a hub of modern Nordic culture, is also a gateway to the country's Viking past, prominently displayed in museums and in the old sagas told and retold across generations.
- **Adventure and Activities:**
- The rugged Icelandic terrain offers endless possibilities for adventure sports and outdoor activities. Hiking, glacier tours, horseback riding, and whale watching are just a few of the activities that attract thrill-seekers and nature enthusiasts alike.
- **Accessibility and Isolation:**
- Iceland's location makes it an attractive destination for those in both North America and Europe, with direct flights commonly taking only about 3 to 6 hours from most major cities in these regions. Despite this accessibility, Iceland still offers a sense of remote, rugged isolation that is increasingly rare in the world.
- **Northern Lights:**
- One of the most compelling reasons to visit Iceland is the chance to witness the Aurora Borealis, or Northern Lights. This stunning natural light display is best viewed during the winter months in areas away from city lights, offering a magical experience that draws visitors from around the globe.

Now, dear reader, before we plunge headlong into the culinary delights and social customs of this frigid utopia, let's take a moment to familiarize ourselves with the lay of the land. I say, I've seen maps that are less complicated than a spider web, and yet, they still manage to confound me. But, fear not! For this map of Iceland, I assure you, is as straightforward as a Sunday sermon.

Imagine, if you will, a landmass shaped somewhat like a lopsided teardrop - or perhaps a dragon's egg, if you're the whimsical sort. That, my friend, is Iceland. It's not a large country by any means, but it's got more character packed into its 40,000 square miles than a Dickens novel.

Let's start with Reykjavik, the capital city, nestled in the southwest corner like a well-loved teddy bear in a child's arms. It's a vibrant hub of culture, cuisine, and conviviality. With its delightful jumble of colorful buildings, it looks like a rainbow got trapped on land, got tired of the chase, and decided to settle down.

Travel east along the southern coast and you'll find yourself in the realm of the Vikings - the South Region. Here, you'll find a landscape so dramatically beautiful, it could serve as a backdrop for a Wagner opera. Home to the famous Golden Circle, it's a treasure trove of geysers, waterfalls, and hot springs.

Now, mosey on up north and you'll find the Westfjords. It's as remote as it gets, folks! A place where nature still holds dominion over man, and the Northern Lights dance across the sky like celestial debutantes at a ball.

Circle back down and you'll find yourself in the East Region. It's a place that's as quiet as a church mouse, but don't be fooled. It's home to some of the most stunning fjords and charming little fishing villages you'll ever have the pleasure of laying your eyes upon.

Finally, the Highlands, right in the middle of it all - a wild, untamed wilderness that's as rugged as an old cowboy and twice as mysterious. It's hard to reach, but boy, is it worth it!

As for the rest of the country, well, it's filled to the brim with glaciers, volcanoes, and more natural beauty than you can shake a stick at. The Ring Road, a tarmac ribbon that circumnavigates the country, serves as your guiding path through this frozen wonderland.

Planning Your Trip

Now, my good friend, before you pack your bags and head off to Iceland, there are some things you ought to know. Planning your trip to this majestic land of fire and ice, is much like preparing for a dinner party. You wouldn't serve your guests burnt toast and tepid water, would you? No, you'd want to serve them the finest wine and the most succulent roast. Similarly, you wouldn't want to show up in Iceland in the middle of winter with nothing but a Hawaiian shirt and flip flops, would you?

Firstly, timing is everything. Iceland, much like my Aunt Mildred's mood, can be unpredictable. The summer months, from June to August, are the most popular for tourists. The days are longer, and the weather is generally more forgiving than my Aunt Mildred. But don't be fooled, summer in Iceland is not like summer in, say, Florida. So, leave your swimsuits and sunscreen at home. Instead, pack layers of clothing. You'll need them for the cool summer days and the chilly nights.

If you're a fan of the darker side of the day, or if you're partial to a bit of winter wonder, then visit between November and February. This is when you have the best chance of seeing the Northern Lights. Just remember, it's also when Iceland becomes a real-life winter wonderland, so pack your warmest clothes. You wouldn't want to get frostbite on your nose, would you?

When it comes to accommodation, Iceland offers a wide range of options. From fancy hotels in Reykjavik to quaint little cottages in the countryside. My advice? Mix it up a bit. Spend a few nights in the city, soaking up the culture and the nightlife. Then, head out to the countryside, where you can enjoy the peace and quiet, and maybe even see a few elves. Yes, you heard me right. Elves. Many Icelanders believe in them, and who am I to argue?

Now, let's talk about food. Iceland has a unique culinary scene. It's not every day that you get to eat fermented shark or sheep's head, is it? But don't let that scare you. The country also offers more familiar dishes, like lamb and seafood, and let's not forget the famous Icelandic hot dogs. They're a must-try.

Transportation in Iceland can be a bit tricky, especially if you plan to explore the more remote areas. Renting a car is an option, but remember, the roads can be as treacherous as a game of poker with a card shark. Make sure you're comfortable with driving in unpredictable weather conditions.

And finally, make sure you respect the land. Iceland is a beautiful country, but it's also fragile. Stick to marked paths, don't litter, and definitely don't take any rocks home as souvenirs. The elves wouldn't like that.

1 Timing Your Visit:
- **Peak Season (June-August):** Enjoy the best weather, access to all regions, and full tourist services. Ideal for hiking, bird watching, and experiencing the midnight sun.
- **Off-Peak Season (September-May):** Fewer tourists and lower prices. Winter months are optimal for viewing the Northern Lights and participating in snow-related activities.

2 Travel Documentation:
- **Passports:** Must be valid for at least six months after your planned departure from Iceland.
- **Visas:** Check if you need a Schengen visa depending on your nationality. Visit the Icelandic Directorate of Immigration website for the latest requirements.

3 Booking Flights and Accommodations:
- **Flights:** Book at least 3-6 months in advance for the best rates, especially during peak season. Consider flying into Keflavík International Airport.
- **Accommodations:** Options range from luxury hotels in Reykjavik to guesthouses and campgrounds nationwide. Early booking is crucial during summer and around Christmas.

4 Transportation on the Island:
- **Car Rentals:** Essential for flexible travel. Four-wheel drives are recommended for winter travel or if exploring the Highlands. Book several months ahead for the best selection and prices.
- **Public Transport:** Buses operate in Reykjavik and major towns; however, service to remote areas is limited. Check schedules in advance, especially outside of summer.

5 Itinerary Considerations:

- **Duration:** Most travelers spend 7-10 days, which is suitable for exploring the Golden Circle and the South Coast up to Jökulsárlón.
- **Must-See Locations:** Allocate 2-3 days for Reykjavik, a day each for the Golden Circle and the Blue Lagoon, and additional days for exploring the North or the remote Westfjords.

6 Packing for Icelandic Weather:

- **Clothing:** Weather can be unpredictable; pack waterproof and windproof jackets, thermal layers, and good quality hiking boots.
- **Gear:** Include sunglasses and sunscreen for summer; thermal gloves, hats, and scarves for winter. Don't forget a swimsuit for geothermal pools.

7 Financial Planning:

- **Currency Exchange:** Obtain some Icelandic króna for small purchases. Most places accept credit cards.
- **Daily Budget:** Expect to spend around 12,000 ISK per day as a budget traveler, more if dining out frequently or booking tours.

8 Health and Insurance:

- **Travel Insurance:** Ensure it covers medical expenses, emergency evacuation, and trip cancellation.
- **Medical Facilities:** Well-equipped in major towns; more limited in remote areas.

9 Communication:

- **Cellular Service:** SIM cards are available at the airport or in Reykjavik for widespread coverage.
- **Language:** Icelandic is the official language; English is widely spoken, especially in tourist areas.

10 Respecting Local Culture and Environment:

- **Nature Conservation:** Stick to marked trails to preserve delicate ecosystems.
- **Cultural Sensitivity:** Be aware of local customs and laws; for instance, public intoxication is frowned upon.

Chapter 2
Preparing for Your Travel

BEST TIME TO VISIT

Best Time to Visit Iceland

Choosing when to visit Iceland hinges on your interests, preferred activities, and tolerance for varying weather conditions. Here's a concise guide to help you decide the best time for your trip:

1 Summer (June to August):
- **Weather:** Warmest months with temperatures ranging from 10°C to 15°C. Long daylight hours, with up to 24 hours of daylight around the summer solstice in June.
- **Activities:** Ideal for hiking, bird watching (especially puffins), whale watching, and exploring the Highlands.
- **Events:** Vibrant festival season including National Day (June 17), and various music and cultural festivals.
- **Considerations:** Peak tourist season, resulting in higher prices and more crowded attractions.

2 Autumn (September to October):
- **Weather:** Cooler with temperatures from 4°C to 10°C. Diminishing daylight, vibrant fall colors in September, increasing chances of Northern Lights by late October.
- **Activities:** Great for sightseeing, hot spring visits, and enjoying the less crowded tourist spots.

- **Considerations:** Weather can be unpredictable, with some services in remote areas beginning to close down for the season.

3 Winter (November to March):

- **Weather:** Cold, with temperatures often below freezing, ranging from -1°C to 3°C. Limited daylight hours, especially around the December solstice.
- **Activities:** Prime time for Northern Lights, ice cave tours, snowmobiling, and skiing.
- **Events:** Christmas and New Year festivities are particularly magical with Reykjavik's extensive light displays.
- **Considerations:** Some roads and regions (like the Highlands) are inaccessible. Winter tires and 4x4 vehicles are essential for driving.

4 Spring (April to May):

- **Weather:** Transitioning with temperatures between 0°C and 10°C. Increasing daylight and melting snow revealing fresh landscapes.
- **Activities:** Ideal for those looking to avoid the larger crowds of summer while enjoying activities like whale watching and late-season skiing.
- **Considerations:** Weather can still be quite variable; layered clothing is recommended.

General Travel Tips:

- **Book Early:** Especially if traveling in summer or over the holidays, to secure the best rates and availability.
- **Check Local Guides:** For up-to-date information on road conditions and weather forecasts, especially if traveling in shoulder or winter seasons.
- **Prepare for All Weathers:** Weather can change rapidly in Iceland; packing waterproofs and layers is essential regardless of the season.

In the realm of travel, there's a time for everything. A time for bundling up in woolen sweaters and a time for basking in the sun. A time for catching the Northern Lights and a time for frolicking under the midnight sun. The trick is, my dear reader, to know when to do what. In the case of Iceland, that's a conundrum worthy of a Norse saga.

Now, if you fancy yourself a modern-day Viking, yearning to conquer the icy wilderness, then the winter months might be your cup of hot chocolate. From November to February, Iceland becomes an enchanting winter wonderland, complete with snow-capped mountains, frosted landscapes, and the ethereal dance of the Northern Lights. But mind you, winter in Iceland isn't exactly a walk in the park. The days are short, the nights are long, and the temperature often drops below freezing. Not to mention, the roads can be as slippery as a politician's promises.

On the other hand, if your idea of adventure doesn't involve chattering teeth and layers of thermal wear, then you might want to consider the summer months.

From June to August, Iceland is bathed in nearly 24 hours of daylight, a phenomenon fondly known as the midnight sun. It's a splendid time for hiking, bird-watching, and getting up close and personal with Iceland's famous puffins. The weather is milder, the roads are clearer, and the landscapes are greener than a leprechaun's wardrobe.

However, let's not forget the shoulder seasons of spring and autumn. These months offer a delicate balance of light and dark, cold and warm, and most importantly, fewer tourists. If you're the kind of traveler who detests jostling elbow-to-elbow with camera-toting sightseers, then these might be your golden ticket. Plus, the airfares and accommodations are usually cheaper than a thrift store sale.

But, dear reader, let me remind you that Iceland is as unpredictable as a cat on a hot tin roof. The weather can change faster than a chameleon on a rainbow, and what starts as a sunny day can quickly turn into a snowstorm. So, no matter when you choose to visit, pack your suitcases with a dash of flexibility and a healthy dose of patience.

So, when's the best time to visit Iceland? Well, that's like asking what's the best way to eat a potato. It all depends on your taste, your appetite, and how much you're willing to brave the elements. Whether you're a winter warrior or a summer sun-seeker, Iceland has a season for you. Just remember to pack your sense of humor along with your woolen socks and sunscreen. After all, you're in the land of sagas and trolls, where every day is an adventure and every season is a story waiting to be told.

Cost And Budgeting

Well now, let's talk about the moolah, the greenbacks, the dough - in simpler terms, let's get down to the brass tacks of cost and budgeting for your Icelandic adventure. Now, don't get your britches in a twist. Iceland, like a high-maintenance belle at the ball, can be a tad expensive. But with a little wit and wisdom, you can still have a grand ol' time without selling the farm.

First off, food ain't cheap in this frosty paradise. You might reckon that a bowl of soup would cost as much as a loaf of bread back home, but you'd be wrong. A bowl of traditional lamb soup, as warming as a grandma's hug on a cold day, will set you back a pretty penny. But it's worth every cent, I assure you. And if you're feeling a bit adventurous, you can try the fermented shark - a delicacy that's as unique as a three-legged dog, but not for the faint-hearted or the weak-stomached.

Now, as for accommodations, if you're expecting a palace for the price of a pigsty, you're in for a surprise. Decent lodgings in Reykjavik can cost a small fortune, but if you're willing to bunk with a few strangers in a hostel, you can save a few bucks. Or, if you're the outdoorsy type, you can always pitch a tent and sleep under the stars - just make sure you're not trespassing on a troll's territory!

Transportation can be another wallet-drainer. Renting a car is a popular choice, but remember, fuel prices in Iceland are as high as a cat's back. If you're not planning on venturing far from the city, public transportation is your best bet. Buses are as dependable as an old mule, and if you're lucky, you might even share your ride with a Viking or two.

But let's not forget about the main attraction - the breathtaking natural wonders. Most of these are as free as a bird, but some, like the Blue Lagoon, will require you to dig deep into your pockets. It's a once-in-a-lifetime experience, though, as soothing as a warm bath on a winter's night.

Now, if you're a bit of a Scrooge, you can save a few pennies by cooking your meals, avoiding the tourist traps, and sticking to the free attractions. But remember, you're in Iceland, a country as beautiful and unique as a snowflake. So, loosen those purse strings a little and enjoy all that this frosty paradise has to offer.

Here's a detailed breakdown of typical costs and budgeting tips to help you plan your financials for the trip:

1 Flights:

• **Cost:** Depends on departure location and season. Flights from the US or Europe can range from $300 to $800 for economy round-trip.

• **Tips:** Book in advance and monitor airline deals. Consider flying during shoulder seasons for better rates.

2 Accommodations:

• **Cost:** Ranges widely depending on type:

• Budget (hostels, guesthouses): $50 to $100 per night.

• Mid-range (hotels, B&Bs): $150 to $250 per night.

• Luxury (top hotels, private lodges): $300 and above per night.

• **Tips:** Book early, especially for summer travel. Consider alternative accommodations like farm stays or renting apartments.

3 Transportation:

• **Car Rental:** $50 to $120 per day, depending on the car type and season.

• **Gasoline:** Approximately $1.80 to $2.20 per liter.

• **Public Transportation:** Buses in Reykjavik start at about $3 per ride; multi-day passes and regional bus tours are also available.

• **Tips:** Rent a car for flexibility; consider sharing the rental with others to split costs. Check for inclusive packages with unlimited mileage and insurance.

4 Food and Dining:

• **Cost:** Eating out is generally pricey.

• Budget meal: $15 to $25.

- Mid-range restaurant meal: $25 to $50.
- High-end dining: $50 and above.
- **Groceries:** Budget about $50 to $70 per week for self-catering.
- **Tips:** Cook when possible, as dining out frequently can be costly. Look for combo meals and lunch specials in restaurants for better value.

5 Activities and Tours:

- **Cost:** Varies by activity.
- Guided tours (Golden Circle, South Coast): $50 to $150.
- Adventure activities (glacier hiking, whale watching): $100 to $250.
- Museums and cultural sites: $10 to $30 entry.
- **Tips:** Prioritize activities based on interests; book tours in advance for discounts. Consider purchasing a city pass in Reykjavik for savings on attractions.

6 Miscellaneous:

- **Souvenirs:** Range from $10 for small items like keychains to $100 and up for quality woolens and crafts.
- **Internet:** Free Wi-Fi is common in hotels and cafes.
- **Tips:** Set aside a budget for unexpected expenses like extra gear or impromptu excursions.

Overall Daily Budget:

- **Economy:** $100 to $150 per day.
- **Moderate:** $200 to $350 per day.
- **Luxury:** $400 and above per day.

Budgeting Tips:

- **Travel Off-Peak:** Reduce costs significantly by visiting in the shoulder months (April, May, September, October).
- **Bundle Services:** Look for package deals that include flights, accommodation, and car rental.
- **Manage Expectations:** Be prepared for high prices and budget extra for unforeseen expenses to ensure a stress-free trip.

What To Pack

If you're planning a jaunt to Iceland, it's crucial to remember that the weather there is as unpredictable as a cat on a hot tin roof, and just as liable to change its mind. Therefore, the first rule of packing for Iceland is to anticipate capricious meteorological conditions.

Firstly, you might be thinking, 'I'll just pack my warmest coat and be done with it'. Well, I hate to burst your bubble, but that's akin to bringing a knife to a gunfight. Iceland's weather isn't just cold, it's a merry mix of wind, rain, snow, sleet, and on the off chance, sunshine. Thus, your packing list should be more comprehensive than just a winter coat.

Now, let's talk about clothing. You'll need to pack layers, and I don't mean just a couple of flannel shirts. Think in terms of thermal underwear, woolen sweaters, and waterproof jackets and pants. These are your best bet against the Icelandic elements. Remember, it's better to be looking at it than looking for it.

Footwear is another crucial aspect. You need boots that can handle not only the cold but also the terrain. The Icelandic landscape is as varied as a patchwork quilt, ranging from volcanic rock to glacier ice. Your footwear should be sturdy, waterproof, and comfortable enough for long walks or hikes.

Don't forget your accessories! Gloves, scarves, hats, and even thermal socks are not just fashion statements but necessities in Iceland's climate. And if you're planning on taking a dip in one of those geothermal pools, pack a swimsuit. It might seem counterintuitive, but it's true. Even in the land of fire and ice, there's a chance for a warm soak.

Packing the right gear is important, but so is packing the right attitude. Iceland is a land of stark contrasts and breathtaking beauty. It's a place where the Northern Lights dance across the sky and geysers erupt from the earth with a fury. It's a place where you can walk between continental plates and watch whales breach in the bay.

In the midst of all this, remember to pack your sense of adventure. Be prepared to marvel at the midnight sun, to feel the spray of the mighty Gullfoss waterfall on your face, to taste the unique flavor of fermented shark if you dare.

Also, don't forget to pack your patience. Things in Iceland may not always go according to plan. Weather conditions can change rapidly, roads can get closed, and tours can get cancelled. But don't let these minor inconveniences dampen your spirits.

Lastly, pack your respect for nature. Iceland is a country that takes conservation seriously. Stick to marked trails, don't litter, and respect the wildlife. Remember, you're a guest in their home.

And remember, as the old Icelandic saying goes, 'There is no such thing as bad weather, only bad clothing.' So pack smart, pack right, and get ready to explore the land of fire and ice.

1 Clothing:

• **Layering is Key:** Start with moisture-wicking base layers (thermal underwear), add insulating mid-layers (fleece or wool sweaters), and top with a waterproof and windproof outer layer (jacket and pants).

• **Footwear:** Waterproof hiking boots for exploring rugged terrains and comfortable walking shoes for urban areas.

- **Accessories:** Warm hats, gloves, and scarves for cold weather. Don't forget a good pair of sunglasses and a sunhat for brighter days.

2 Outdoor Gear:

- **Backpack:** A sturdy daypack is essential for carrying snacks, water, and extra clothing while on excursions.
- **Water Bottle:** Stay hydrated during long outings; tap water is safe to drink and delicious in Iceland.
- **Swimwear:** Include a swimsuit for visits to hot springs and public pools, along with a quick-dry towel.

3 Technical Items:

- **Travel Adapters:** Iceland uses type C and F plugs, with a standard voltage of 230 V and 50 Hz.
- **Mobile Devices:** Bring your smartphone and charger; consider a portable power bank for long days out.
- **Camera Gear:** Pack a good camera with extra batteries to capture the stunning landscapes. A waterproof case or bag may be helpful.

4 Health and Safety:

- **First Aid Kit:** Include basic first aid supplies along with any personal medications.
- **Sunscreen and Lip Balm:** Even in cold weather, sun protection is important, especially when snow or water reflects UV rays.
- **Insect Repellent:** Useful during the summer months in certain areas.

5 Navigation Tools:

- **Maps and Guidebooks:** Even if you plan to use digital navigation, having physical maps can be helpful.
- **GPS or Smartphone Apps:** Ensure you have offline maps downloaded or GPS devices ready for areas with limited cell service.

6 Miscellaneous:

- **Travel Insurance Documents:** Keep a copy of your travel insurance details handy.
- **Snacks:** Energy bars, nuts, or chocolate can be great for a quick energy boost during activities.
- **Reusable Shopping Bag:** Handy for grocery shopping, as plastic bags are often charged.

7 Cultural Items:

- **Phrasebook or Language App:** While English is widely spoken, having some Icelandic phrases can enhance interactions with locals.
- **Travel Journal:** Keep a diary or a journal to record your experiences and memories.

Travel Insurance Essentials

Now, if you're anything like me, you might have a tendency to skip over the dull, practical details of planning a trip. You might be thinking, 'Insurance? Bah, I don't need no stinkin' insurance! I'm as tough as a Viking and twice as brave!' Well, hold your horses, my friend. Even the toughest Viking wouldn't set sail without ensuring he had a sturdy hull and a sharp axe. And that, in essence, is what travel insurance is all about.

So, let's talk about this mysterious beast called travel insurance. Now, I know it's not as exciting as the Northern Lights or as tantalizing as a bowl of hákarl, but bear with me. It's a necessary evil, like wearing socks with sandals or eating your vegetables. Your mother was right about those, wasn't she?

First off, let's clear the air. Travel insurance is not some magical shield that protects you from all mishap and misadventure. It's more like a safety net, there to catch you when you stumble. It's there to cover the costs of unforeseen circumstances that might befall you on your journey, like a sudden illness, a lost suitcase, or a missed flight because you were too busy trying to pronounce Eyjafjallajökull.

Now, let's talk about the types of travel insurance. There's trip cancellation insurance, which covers you if you have to cancel your trip for a covered reason, like a sudden illness or a volcanic eruption. Then there's travel health insurance, which is a must-have if you plan on wrestling with any Icelandic trolls or eating fermented shark. Trust me, your stomach will thank you.

And don't forget about baggage insurance. If you've ever had the misfortune of losing your suitcase in the wilds of an airport, you'll know the value of this. It covers you if your luggage is lost, delayed, or damaged. And if you're planning on bringing along any expensive equipment, like a fancy camera to capture those beautiful geysers, you might want to consider getting additional coverage.

Now, you might be thinking, 'But I'm a careful traveler! I never lose my luggage, I always eat healthy, and I certainly don't wrestle trolls!' Well, good for you. But let me tell you a little secret. Even the most careful travelers can encounter unexpected surprises. Like that one time I found myself stranded on a glacier with nothing but a pocket knife and a bag of dried fish. But that's a story for another time.

The point is, you never know what might happen. And that's what makes travel exciting! But it's also what makes travel insurance essential. So, before you set off on your Icelandic adventure, make sure you're properly covered. It might not be as thrilling as riding an Icelandic horse or bathing in a hot spring, but it will give you peace of mind. And that, my friend, is priceless.

1 Travel Insurance:
- **Coverage:** Look for a policy that covers trip cancellation, trip interruption,

lost luggage, and missed connections. Consider the financial limits and exclusions to ensure they meet your needs.

- **Medical Coverage:** Ensure your policy includes comprehensive medical insurance, covering emergency medical treatment, hospital stays, and potentially emergency evacuation. This is particularly important given the adventurous activities and remote locations you may explore in Iceland.

2 Car Rental Insurance:

- **Collision Damage Waiver (CDW) and Super CDW:** These reduce your liability in case of damage to the rental vehicle. Note that gravel protection is also advisable due to Iceland's many gravel roads.
- **Theft Protection:** While vehicle theft is not common in Iceland, having theft protection can add an extra layer of security.

3 Activity-Specific Insurance:

- If you plan to engage in high-risk activities like glacier hiking, ice climbing, or off-roading, check that your travel insurance policy covers these specifically. Some policies require additional coverage for such activities.

4 Health Insurance:

- **EHIC/GHIC Cards:** For European travelers, an European Health Insurance Card (EHIC) or a Global Health Insurance Card (GHIC) can provide access to necessary healthcare services during your stay, similar to what you would receive at home.
- **Global Travelers:** Ensure that your health insurance is valid internationally and includes coverage for Iceland. Check if you need to notify your provider about your travel plans.

5 Cancellation Insurance:

- Given the unpredictable nature of Iceland's weather, which can lead to sudden changes in travel plans, having cancellation insurance can be particularly beneficial.

Tips for Buying Insurance:

- **Read the Fine Print:** Understand what is and is not covered, especially regarding the weather and activity exclusions.
- **Buy Early:** Purchase your travel insurance shortly after booking your trip to ensure coverage for pre-trip issues that might cause cancellation.
- **Keep Documentation:** Carry proof of your insurance policies with you and keep digital copies accessible in case you need to reference them or make a claim while abroad.

Chapter 3

Before You Go

VISA AND ENTRY REQUIREMENTS

Ah, the grandeur of Iceland, a land of fire and ice, with its majestic fjords, glistening glaciers, and the occasional puffin. But before you can set foot on this rugged, beautiful terrain, you need to navigate the intricate labyrinth that is the visa and entry requirements. Fear not, dear traveler, for I am here to guide you through this bureaucratic maze with a dash of humor and a sprinkle of social charm.

Now, the good news for those fortunate folks hailing from the Schengen Area, you have been bestowed the privilege of free movement. That's right, you can waltz right into Iceland without the need for a visa. You can thank the powers-that-be for this convenience. But remember, while you're enjoying the Northern Lights or soaking in the Blue Lagoon, don't forget to carry your passport or ID card. Iceland may be forgiving, but it's not forgetful.

For our friends across the pond in the United States, Canada, and numerous other countries, you enjoy the privilege of visa-free travel for up to 90 days within a 180-day period. Not too shabby, eh? But don't get too excited and pack your bags just yet. You'll need to ensure your passport is valid for at least three months beyond your planned departure date. Iceland, while being a land of myths and legends, is not particularly fond of mythical travelers with expired passports.

For those who aren't as lucky, fear not. Iceland, being the friendly nation that it is, has a visa application process that is as warm and welcoming as its geothermal hot springs. You'll need to apply for a Schengen visa at the nearest

Icelandic embassy or consulate in your home country. The process involves a bit of paperwork, a smidgen of patience, and a dash of good humor. Don't forget to bring along a couple of passport-sized photos (the kind where you're not allowed to smile – a bit of a paradox in this land of happiness, isn't it?).

Once you've secured your visa, you're almost ready to experience the magic of Iceland. But hold your horses there, traveler. Iceland has a few entry requirements up its woolly sleeve. You'll need to show proof of sufficient funds to support yourself during your stay. Now, 'sufficient' is a relative term. It doesn't mean you need to own an oil well or a gold mine. A few thousand kronas should do the trick.

And lastly, but most importantly, you must present a return or onward ticket. Iceland is a beautiful place, no doubt, but they do like their visitors to eventually leave. It's nothing personal, just a bit of island housekeeping.

1 Schengen Agreement:
- **Visa-Free Travel:** Iceland is part of the Schengen Agreement, allowing citizens of other Schengen countries to enter visa-free for up to 90 days in any 180-day period.
- **Non-Schengen Countries:** Citizens from the United States, Canada, Australia, and several other countries can also enter Iceland without a visa for tourist visits of up to 90 days.

2 Visa Requirements:
- **Who Needs a Visa:** Travelers from countries not under the visa exemption agreement with the Schengen Zone must apply for a Schengen visa. This includes countries like India, China, and Russia, among others.
- **Application Process:** Visa applications should be submitted to the nearest Icelandic consulate or an embassy representing Iceland in visa matters. The process typically involves submitting a completed application form, passport-size photos, travel itinerary, proof of accommodation, travel insurance, and a visa fee.
- **Processing Time:** It's advisable to apply at least 15 working days before the planned trip, though processing times can vary.

3 Entry Requirements:
- **Valid Passport:** All visitors to Iceland must hold a passport valid for at least three months beyond their planned departure date from the Schengen area.
- **Proof of Financial Means:** Travelers may need to demonstrate they have sufficient funds to cover their stay in Iceland. This is usually around 4,000 ISK (approximately 30 USD) per day.
- **Return Ticket:** Although not always checked, having proof of a return or onward ticket can be required under certain circumstances.

4 Customs Regulations:
- **Duty-Free Allowances:** Iceland allows a certain amount of duty-free goods, which includes alcohol and tobacco, within specified limits.

- **Restricted Items:** Certain items such as raw foods, weapons, and large amounts of currency must be declared upon entry. Always check the latest customs regulations before traveling.

5 Health and Safety:

- **Vaccinations:** No special vaccinations are required for Iceland. However, it's wise to be up-to-date with routine vaccinations.

- **COVID-19 Regulations:** As health regulations can change, verify the current COVID-19 entry requirements before traveling. This may include vaccination certificates, negative tests, or quarantine mandates.

6 Staying Longer:

- **Extended Stays and Residency:** For stays longer than 90 days, or for purposes such as work or study, a different type of visa or residence permit is required. Applications for these permits should be made through the Directorate of Immigration in Iceland.

Tips for Smooth Entry:

- **Documentation:** Keep all necessary documents handy, including insurance, accommodation proof, and return tickets.

- **Check Updates:** Immigration rules can change. Always check the Icelandic Directorate of Immigration's website or consult the embassy for the most current information prior to your departure.

Health And Safety Advice

Now, let's take a moment to talk about health and safety, a topic as riveting as watching wet paint dry, yet as necessary as a woolen sweater in an Icelandic snowstorm.

Firstly, we must discuss the local cuisine. Now, I don't want to frighten you, but the Icelandic folks have a particular fondness for dishes that might make your stomach quiver. Fermented shark, boiled sheep's head, and pickled ram's testicles are just a few of the delicacies on offer. If you have a weak constitution or are a staunch vegetarian, it might be best to stick to the local bread and butter. Literally.

However, if you're the adventurous type, by all means, dive right into these culinary wonders. Just remember, if you find yourself turning a peculiar shade of green, it's not the Northern Lights. It's your stomach protesting.

Speaking of the Northern Lights, they are a sight to behold. But do remember, while you're craning your neck skywards, watch your footing. The Icelandic terrain is as unpredictable as a cat on catnip. One moment you're on solid ground, the next you're knee-deep in a snowdrift.

Now, let's move on to the geysers. They're as temperamental as a teapot on a hot stove. They might seem calm and serene, but they can erupt without warning. So, keep a respectful distance, unless you fancy a hot shower in public.

Iceland is also famous for its glaciers. But remember, while they might look as sturdy as a Viking warrior, they're as unstable as a house of cards. So, tread lightly, and don't go wandering off the beaten path. That's the quickest way to find yourself in a crevasse, and trust me, that's not a place you want to be.

As for the Icelandic weather, it's as changeable as a chameleon in a rainbow. One moment it's sunny and bright, the next it's snowing like there's no tomorrow. So, dress in layers. And I mean layers. Think of it as a culinary lasagna, each layer providing warmth and protection against the elements.

Lastly, let's talk about the Icelandic wildlife. The most dangerous creature you'll likely encounter is a puffin. These adorable birds are as harmless as a newborn lamb. But do keep your distance. They're not fond of selfies, and they have a wicked peck.

In all seriousness though, your safety is paramount. So, heed local advice, respect the environment, and remember, it's better to be safe than sorry. After all, you're here to enjoy yourself, not to win a Darwin award.

1 Medical Facilities:
- **Access:** Urban areas are well-equipped with medical facilities, while remote regions have limited services. It's advisable to know the location of the nearest clinic or hospital relative to your travel itinerary.
- **Insurance:** Ensure you have comprehensive travel health insurance that covers medical treatment abroad and, if necessary, medical evacuation.

2 Vaccinations:
- **Routine Vaccines:** Be up-to-date with routine vaccinations such as measles, mumps, rubella (MMR), diphtheria-tetanus-pertussis, varicella (chickenpox), polio, and your yearly flu shot.

3 Water Safety:
- **Drinking Water:** Tap water is safe to drink and of high quality. There's no need to buy bottled water, which helps reduce plastic use.

4 Road Safety:
- **Driving Conditions:** Be prepared for rapidly changing weather conditions that can impact driving. Always use seat belts and avoid off-road driving unless in a suitable vehicle and area where it is permitted.
- **Legal Requirements:** A valid driving license from your country is required, and an International Driving Permit is recommended for non-EU license holders.

5 Natural Hazards:
- **Weather:** Weather can change quickly, so dress in layers and always carry waterproof gear.
- **Geothermal and Volcanic Areas:** Respect safety barriers and signage in

geothermal parks and near volcanoes to avoid hazards such as hot springs and unstable ground.

6 Safety Precautions:

- **Hiking and Outdoor Activities:** Use appropriate gear and check the weather forecast before engaging in outdoor activities. Consider using a guide for more challenging terrains.
- **Emergency Numbers:** Familiarize yourself with local emergency contacts. The universal emergency number is 112, accessible from any phone.

7 Personal Security:

- **Low Crime Rate:** Although the destination is known for its safety and low crime rate, always practice common-sense precautions such as safeguarding your belongings and being aware of your environment, especially in tourist-heavy areas.

8 Health Advisory:

- **COVID-19 and Other Diseases:** Stay informed about any health advisories or outbreaks. Adhering to updated health guidelines from global and local health authorities is crucial.

Cultural Etiquette

As we meander through the snowy expanse of this Icelandic guide, it is only fitting that we stumble upon the ice-laden path of cultural etiquette. Now, one must understand that Icelanders are a stoic lot, not given to the frivolous outbursts of emotion that we, the more temperate folk, are accustomed to. They prefer their greetings with a firm handshake, not the effusive hugs and kisses that some of us may be fond of.

Do remember, dear reader, that when you're exchanging names with an Icelander, they might introduce themselves with their first name, followed by their father's first name, with a dash of 'son' or 'dóttir' added for good measure. It's a charming little quirk of theirs, and it's best to follow suit.

Now, punctuality is a virtue that Icelanders hold dear. If you've been invited to a social gathering, don't saunter in fashionably late. It is considered disrespectful. But don't be too early either; they value their personal time. Aim for the sweet spot, right on the dot.

And when it comes to dining, Icelanders are a relaxed bunch. They don't stand on ceremony, but they do appreciate good manners. Always remember to say 'Takk fyrir mig' (Thanks for me) after a meal. It's a simple phrase that goes a long way in earning you brownie points with your hosts.

Speaking of meals, you may find yourself face to face with some curious Icelandic delicacies. Don't look so aghast, dear reader! Remember, when in

Rome, do as the Romans do. So when in Iceland, don't shy away from the fermented shark or the sheep's head. They might not be your cup of tea, but a little adventurous indulgence never hurt anyone.

Now, let's talk about the geothermal pools. They're a cornerstone of Icelandic culture and a must-visit for any traveler. But remember, cleanliness is next to godliness and Icelanders take this very seriously. Shower thoroughly before you dip into these pools. It's not just good manners, it's the law!

Don't be surprised if you see Icelanders casually conversing with each other in the nude in the changing rooms. They're not being exhibitionists; they're just comfortable in their own skin. If you're not, just keep your gaze firmly fixed on the horizon, and you'll be fine.

1 Greetings and Interactions:

- **Formality:** Initially, interactions are polite and reserved. Use titles and last names unless invited to use first names.
- **Personal Space:** Maintain a respectful distance during conversations. Physical contact is minimal, usually limited to handshakes.

2 Dining Etiquette:

- **Invitations:** If invited to a home, bring a small gift such as flowers, chocolates, or wine.
- **Table Manners:** Wait until the host invites you to start eating. Compliment the food and finish what is on your plate as a sign of appreciation.
- **Tipping:** Tipping is not customary; service charges are typically included in the bill.

3 Communication Style:

- **Directness:** Communication is direct but not blunt. Honesty is valued, but being tactful is equally important.
- **Punctuality:** Time is respected; arrive on time for appointments and social gatherings.

4 Dress Code:

- **General Attire:** Dress is casual but neat. For business or formal events, a more conservative approach is typical.
- **Outdoor Activities:** Wear appropriate gear for outdoor activities. Practicality and safety are prioritized over fashion.

5 Public Behavior:

- **Respect for Nature:** Show respect for the environment by sticking to marked trails, not littering, and avoiding disturbance to wildlife.
- **Alcohol Consumption:** Public intoxication is frowned upon. Consume alcohol responsibly.

6 Swimming Pools and Spas:

- **Hygiene:** Shower without swimwear before entering pools or spas, as cleanliness is taken very seriously.
- **Behavior:** Speak quietly and relax; these areas are not typically places for loud conversations or boisterous behavior.

7 Photography:

- **Privacy:** Ask for permission before taking photos of people, especially in rural areas. Respect signs or requests for no photography, particularly in cultural sites.

Sustainable Travel Tips

Now, my fine fellow travelers, let us turn our attention to a topic of undeniable importance - the art of sustainable traveling within the fair lands of Iceland. Now, don't you go rolling your eyes at me! This isn't some high-minded lecture about saving the whales or hugging the trees (though both worthy endeavors, I must say). No, this is about making sure the land of fire and ice stays as pristine and unspoiled as it was when the Vikings first laid their eyes on it.

Now, the first thing you must remember is to treat Iceland as you would a delicate maiden. Be gentle, be respectful, and for the love of all things holy, don't leave your trash lying around! It's a simple act, but one that does wonders in preserving the natural beauty of the place.

Next, let's talk transportation. Now, I know the temptation to rent a big, burly 4x4 and go rampaging through the wilderness like some modern-day conqueror is strong. But resist, dear reader, resist! Instead, opt for public transportation or shared rides. Not only will you save a pretty penny, but you'll also reduce your carbon footprint. And who knows, you might meet some interesting characters along the way.

Speaking of characters, let's talk about the locals. Icelanders are a friendly lot, but like all people, they appreciate it when visitors respect their customs and traditions. So do your homework, learn a few phrases in Icelandic (it's a tongue-twister, I assure you), and try to blend in. Not only will you have a more authentic experience, but you'll also avoid the dreaded label of 'ignorant tourist'.

Now, onto food. Iceland is known for its unique culinary delights, some of which might make the faint-hearted quail. But fear not! The key to sustainable eating is to go local. That means trying out the fermented shark, the dried fish, and yes, even the sheep's head. Not only will your taste buds have an adventure of their own, but you'll also support local farmers and fishermen.

Lastly, let's talk souvenirs. Now, I know the allure of those cute little puffin figurines or the woolen sweaters is strong. But consider this - do you really need them? Most of these trinkets are mass-produced and contribute to the waste problem. Instead, opt for experiences. Go for a dip in the Blue Lagoon, watch the Northern Lights, or hike a glacier. These are memories that will last a lifetime and don't require any extra luggage space.

1 Low-Impact Transportation:

- **Biking and Walking:** Where safe and feasible, opt for biking or walking to explore. Many destinations offer bike rental services with designated paths that provide a scenic and eco-friendly way to see the sights.
- **Ridesharing:** Utilize rideshare apps where public transportation isn't available, which can reduce the number of vehicles on the road and lower your carbon footprint.
- **Vehicle Rentals:** When renting a vehicle, ask for the most fuel-efficient model available. Some rental agencies now offer ultra-efficient or electric vehicles, especially in urban centers.

2 Eco-Friendly Accommodations:

- **Sustainability Practices:** Look for accommodations that practice water conservation, use energy-efficient lighting and appliances, and have effective waste management systems in place.
- **Local Materials and Crafts:** Prefer hotels that incorporate local materials and crafts in their decor, which supports local artisans and reduces the carbon footprint associated with shipping materials from afar.

3 Supporting Local Economies:

- **Volunteering:** Consider dedicating a portion of your trip to volunteering with local organizations that focus on environmental conservation or community aid. This can provide deeper insight into the local culture and the specific challenges it faces.
- **Fair Trade Products:** When shopping, look for fair trade labels to ensure that products are being produced ethically and that producers are paid fair wages.

4 Interaction with Nature and Wildlife:

- **Avoid Disturbance:** Always observe wildlife from a distance, and resist the urge to feed, touch, or interact with wild animals, as this can disturb their natural behaviors and ecosystems.
- **Protected Areas:** Pay entrance fees for national parks and protected areas; these fees are used to fund conservation efforts and maintain the facilities without resorting to more intrusive or damaging forms of revenue.

5 Waste Reduction:

- **Digital Tickets and Receipts:** Opt for digital boarding passes, tickets, and receipts whenever possible to reduce paper use.
- **Packaging:** Avoid products with excessive packaging, particularly plastics. If you must buy packaged goods, choose items packaged in recycled materials.

6 Water Use:

• **Report Leaks:** If you notice a leaking faucet or toilet in your hotel, report it to management as soon as possible to prevent water wastage.

7 Carbon Offsets:

• **Local Projects:** When possible, choose carbon offset projects that also provide benefits to the community where you're traveling, such as reforestation projects or the development of sustainable local businesses.

8 Cultural Sensitivity and Support:

• **Respectful Photography:** Always ask for permission before photographing people, especially in rural or indigenous communities. This shows respect for their privacy and dignity.

• **Supporting Local Arts:** Attend local performances, purchase art directly from the creators, and visit community-run sites, ensuring your money benefits the community directly.

9 Advocacy and Awareness:

• **Educational Experiences:** Engage in tours and experiences that offer education about the local environment or community challenges, which can provide greater context for your travels and inspire more thoughtful interaction with the place.

Chapter 4
Getting There and Around

FLYING TO ICELAND

Now, the first order of business is to secure oneself a ticket on one of those magnificent flying machines. You know, the ones with the wings that seem to defy the laws of gravity? Yes, those ones. There's a host of airlines that'll carry you off to Iceland quicker than you can say 'Eyjafjallajökull'. But do pardon my Icelandic; it's a language that tends to get stuck in one's throat.

Once you've got your ticket in hand, and you've packed your woolly socks, it's time to head to the airport. Now, remember, these aren't your run-of-the-mill train stations. They have peculiar rules about what you can carry and what you can't. It's a good idea to leave your pet alligator and collection of exotic cacti at home. They aren't too fond of those in the luggage compartments, you see.

Up you go into the sky, into the land of fluffy, cotton candy clouds. If you're lucky, you might even catch a glimpse of Greenland, not to be confused with Iceland. One's all ice, and the other's all green. Quite the geographical prank, isn't it? You'll be served a meal or two during your flight, an interesting assortment of food that looks like it's been miniaturized. But worry not, it's perfectly edible, although you might find yourself developing a sudden appreciation for your own cooking.

As your plane descends, you'll witness the rugged beauty of Iceland unfolding beneath you - a patchwork of green and white, stitched together by the silver threads of winding rivers and waterfalls. You'll see the twinkling lights of Reykjavik, the capital city, welcoming you with open arms. It's a sight that'll make your heart flutter, even if you've left your fear of heights back at the airport.

Once you've landed, and the kind folks at the airport have ensured you haven't smuggled in any forbidden fruits or vegetables, you're free to step out into the crisp Icelandic air. Welcome to the land of ice and fire, my dear reader! But beware, the real adventure is just about to begin.

Interesting and Lesser-Known Aspects of Flying to and Exploring Iceland

Continuing on from the thrill of your airborne arrival, here are some captivating tidbits that might surprise and delight you about Iceland and your journey there:

1 Mid-Atlantic Ridge Visibility:

• Iceland is one of the few places in the world where the Mid-Atlantic Ridge is visible above water. As your flight descends, you might catch a glimpse of this geological marvel, especially near the Þingvellir National Park.

2 Iceland's Renewable Energy:

• When flying into Iceland, you may notice large steam plumes rising from the ground. These are from geothermal power plants, which, along with hydroelectric power, provide nearly all of the country's electricity. Iceland is a leader in renewable energy usage.

3 Airport Art and Design:

• Keflavík Airport, your likely point of entry, features architecture and art installations inspired by Icelandic nature. Look out for designs that mimic volcanic landscapes, ocean waves, and the northern lights.

4 Unique Flight Paths:

• Some flights to Iceland offer routes that pass directly over the Arctic Circle. On clear days, this can provide passengers with breathtaking views of the Arctic ice pack or the northern lights, depending on the season.

5 The Proximity of U.S. and European Mainlands:

• Iceland's strategic location makes it a common stopover for transatlantic flights. Some airlines offer a "stopover" program, allowing travelers to explore Iceland for a few days before continuing to their final destination without additional airfare.

6 Flora and Fauna from Above:

• As you descend, keep an eye out for Iceland's rugged coastline and diverse wildlife habitats. You may spot sprawling bird colonies and, during certain seasons, pods of whales near the shores.

7 Volcanic Scenery:

• The aerial view of Iceland's active volcanic landscape is unmatched. Notice the contrast between ancient lava fields, active volcanic craters, and vibrant moss that blankets much of the terrain.

8 Icelandic Horses:

- Upon landing and traveling through the countryside, you might notice small herds of the unique Icelandic horse. Known for their extra gait called the "tölt," these horses have been purebred in Iceland for centuries and are much cherished.

9 Microclimate Observation:

- Iceland is known for its saying, "If you don't like the weather, wait five minutes." The island's diverse microclimates can be fascinating as you might experience sudden changes from sunshine to rain to snow, sometimes visible even from the plane as you approach.

10 The Quietness of Airspace:

- Due to its sparse population and remote location, Iceland's airspace is less congested, which can make for unusually smooth and quiet flights, especially as you approach the island.

Car Rentals And Driving In Iceland

Firstly, let's discuss the matter of procuring a vehicle. The car rental agencies in Iceland are as plentiful as puffins in springtime. You'll find them at the airport, in the city, and dotted about the countryside like daisies in a meadow. They offer an array of vehicles, from the modest economy car to the grand four-wheel-drive SUV. The choice, as they say, is yours. But remember, this is Iceland, a land of glaciers, geysers, and gravel roads. If your itinerary includes any off-the-beaten-path excursions, you might want to consider a vehicle that can handle such rugged terrain.

Now, onto the matter of driving. Driving in Iceland is a bit like being a contestant on a game show. You'll need to be quick on your feet, have a keen eye, and above all, stay calm under pressure. The roads are generally well-maintained, but can be narrow and winding, especially in rural areas. And let's not forget about the weather, which can change faster than a chameleon on a rainbow. One minute it's clear skies and sunshine, the next it's a blizzard that would give a polar bear pause.

There are also a few quirks to Icelandic driving that you'll need to be aware of. For instance, in most places, the right of way is given to the driver coming from the right. But in roundabouts, it's the inside lane that has the right of way. Confusing? Perhaps. But as my grandmother used to say, "When in Rome, do as the Icelanders do."

And speaking of doing as the Icelanders do, let's talk about speed limits. In most urban areas, the limit is 50 km/h, while on rural roads it's 80 km/h, and on highways, it's 90 km/h. But don't take these as mere suggestions. The Icelandic police are quite vigilant, and fines can be hefty. So, unless you've got a pocket full of krona you're itching to part with, I'd advise keeping a steady foot on the pedal.

Now, you might be thinking, "But what about gas stations?" Well, worry not. Gas stations in Iceland are as common as hot springs. And they're not just for fueling your vehicle. Many also offer a selection of snacks, hot meals, and even groceries. So, you can fill your tank and your belly at the same time.

1 Choosing the Right Vehicle:

• **Type of Vehicle:** Consider the nature of your travel itinerary. For summer travel on main roads, a standard car is sufficient. For winter or exploring the Highlands, a four-wheel-drive vehicle is necessary due to rough terrain and potentially harsh weather conditions.

• **Rental Options:** Numerous rental agencies operate at Keflavík International Airport and in Reykjavik. It's advisable to book your vehicle in advance, especially during peak tourist seasons.

2 Legal Requirements:

• **Driving License:** Visitors can drive in Iceland with a valid driver's license from their home country. An International Driving Permit is not required but is recommended for non-European drivers for ease of identification.

• **Age Restrictions:** The minimum age to rent a car typically ranges from 20 to 23 years old, depending on the rental company, with a requirement that the driver has held their license for at least one year. Drivers under 25 may incur a young driver surcharge.

3 Driving Laws:

• **Speed Limits:** Speed limits in Iceland are generally 50 km/h in urban areas, 80 km/h on gravel roads in rural areas, and 90 km/h on paved roads.

• **Seat Belts:** Seat belt use is mandatory for all passengers in the vehicle.

• **Alcohol Limit:** The legal blood alcohol limit is very low at 0.05%. It's best to avoid drinking and driving altogether.

4 Road Conditions:

• **Weather Influences:** Road conditions can vary dramatically with the weather, which can change rapidly. Check the Icelandic Meteorological Office and the Icelandic Road Administration (Vegagerðin) for real-time updates.

• **Off-Road Driving:** Driving off marked roads is illegal in Iceland and can result in heavy fines. This law protects the delicate natural environment from damage.

5 Driving Tips:

• **Headlights:** It's mandatory to keep headlights on at all times, day and night.

- **Fuel:** Keep an eye on your fuel level; gas stations can be sparse in remote areas and many are self-service and require a credit card with a PIN for payment.
- **F Roads:** Only open during summer, these Highland roads require a 4x4 vehicle. Conditions on these roads can be challenging, and they are not maintained in winter.

6 Emergency Numbers:
- **General Emergencies:** Dial 112 for any emergency, a number accessible throughout Iceland.

7 Navigational Tools:
- **GPS and Maps:** While GPS systems are helpful, always carry a physical map as a backup. Mobile service may not be available in remote areas.

8 Insurance:
- **Collision Damage Waiver (CDW):** Typically included with car rentals, this covers damage to the rental car. Consider additional insurance like Gravel Protection (GP), which covers damage from gravel roads, common in Iceland.

Public Transportation Options

Now, let's mosey on over to the delightful world of Icelandic public transportation. You might think it's a dry topic, but I assure you, it's as thrilling as a ride on a bucking bronco and as full of unexpected pleasures as a surprise birthday party.

First, we have the city buses of Reykjavik, painted in a cheerful yellow that could put a sunflower to shame. They're as punctual as a Swiss watch, though I'd advise you not to put too much faith in that. After all, the Icelandic weather is as unpredictable as a cat on a hot tin roof. One minute it's as mild as a lamb, the next, it's blowing a gale fierce enough to whisk you off to Kansas, Dorothy-style. In such situations, even the most punctual bus might get delayed.

Then there's the Strætó app, a technological wonder that lets you track your bus in real time. It's a bit like having a crystal ball, though instead of foreseeing your future, it tells you when your bus is about to arrive. However, let me assure you, it's not a perfect science. Sometimes, the bus marked '2 minutes away' takes its sweet time, moving as slowly as molasses in January. But don't let that ruffle your feathers; it's all part of the adventure.

Now, if you're planning to venture beyond the city, there's no need to hitch up your wagon. The country has a network of long-distance buses that stretch from the rocky shores of Snæfellsnes in the west to the volcanic landscapes of Vatnajökull in the east. These buses are as comfortable as your favorite armchair and as reliable as an old friend. However, their schedules can be as sparse as hen's teeth, especially in the off-peak season. It's always best to check the timetable before you set off, unless you fancy a long wait in the Icelandic wilderness.

For those who are not faint-hearted and have a taste for the high seas, ferries are an excellent option. They chug along the sparkling fjords, offering breath-taking views that could make a poet out of anyone. Just remember, the North Atlantic is not a placid pond. It can get as choppy as a cook's chopping board, so if you're prone to seasickness, it might be wise to keep your feet on solid ground.

1 Buses:

- **City Buses:** In Reykjavik, the city bus service, known as Strætó, offers comprehensive coverage with routes connecting most parts of the city and suburbs. Fares are reasonable, and day passes are available for unlimited travel.

- **Long-Distance Buses:** For travel between towns and other regions, several bus companies operate routes that can take you across the country. The main bus terminal in Reykjavik, BSÍ Bus Terminal, serves as the hub for these services. This includes popular routes like those leading to Akureyri, the Golden Circle, and other tourist destinations.

2 Ferries:

- **Coastal and Island Travel:** Iceland has several ferry services that connect the mainland to the surrounding islands such as Vestmannaeyjar (Westman Islands). Additionally, ferries operate in the Westfjords, providing essential links to remote areas and offering spectacular views during the journey.

3 Domestic Flights:

- **Air Travel within Iceland:** For those looking to save time, domestic flights can be a practical option. Airports in Reykjavik, Akureyri, and Egilsstaðir facilitate quick travel across the country. Airlines like Air Iceland Connect and Eagle Air offer services connecting to smaller towns and regions, making even the most remote areas accessible.

4 Taxis and Rideshare:

- **Taxis:** Available in major towns and cities, taxis can be hailed on the street or ordered via phone. They are metered, and fares are regulated but can be expensive, especially for longer distances.

- **Rideshare Services:** While traditional ridesharing apps like Uber or Lyft are not available, similar services can be found, especially in Reykjavik, through local apps and platforms.

5 Cycling:

- **Biking:** Reykjavik and some other towns are equipped with bike paths, and bicycle rentals are available. Biking can be a pleasant and eco-friendly way to explore urban areas, especially during the milder summer months.

6 Tour Buses:

- **Organized Tours:** For those who prefer not to worry about planning routes and schedules, organized bus tours are available for most popular tourist destinations. These tours often include guided commentary and can provide a deeper understanding of the sights and history of Iceland.

Tips for Using Public Transportation:

• **Planning:** Check schedules in advance as some services may be infrequent, especially outside of peak tourist seasons.

• **Tickets:** Purchase tickets online when possible or through local kiosks and shops. Many bus services offer apps where you can buy tickets and track bus locations in real-time.

• **Weather Considerations:** Always check the weather forecast as it can affect travel plans, especially when using ferries or traveling to more remote areas.

Navigating Icelandic Weather

Firstly, let's discuss the winter, or as I like to call it, "The Season of the Frosty Beard." You see, in the winter, Iceland can get as cold as a landlord's heart. The wind can howl like a pack of wolves, and the snow can fall so thickly you'll think you're inside a snow globe. But, it's not all doom and gloom, no sir. The snow-capped mountains are a sight to behold, and the Northern Lights, why, they'll take your breath away faster than a punch to the gut.

Now, onto the summer, or as I've affectionately named it, "The Season of the Midnight Sun." You see, in the summer, the sun doesn't set. It's like a stubborn mule that refuses to budge. Now, you might think this is a good thing, more daylight to explore, right? Well, let me tell you, it's all fun and games until you're trying to sleep and the sun is still shining brighter than a diamond at midnight.

But, worry not, for I have a few tricks up my sleeve to help you navigate these eccentric weather conditions. For the winter, you'll want to layer up like an onion. And I don't mean just a couple of layers, I mean enough to make you look like the Michelin man. Now, for the summer, invest in a good pair of blackout curtains. Trust me, your sanity will thank you.

Rain in Iceland is as common as fish in the sea. It's not a question of if it will rain, but when. So, always carry an umbrella, or better yet, a waterproof poncho. It might not be the height of fashion, but neither is looking like a drowned rat.

Now, the wind in Iceland is a force to be reckoned with. It's been known to blow tourists clean off their feet. So, if you feel a gust of wind strong enough to blow the hat off a bald man, best to find shelter.

And let's not forget about the sudden fog that can roll in without warning, thicker than pea soup. It's a good idea to always have a compass on hand. Not that it'll help you see through the fog, but at least you'll know which way is north.

Chapter 5

Accommodations

HOW TO CHOOSE WHERE TO STAY

Now, in this rugged country, one might think the only option for housing would be a snow hut or an igloo. Fear not! Iceland offers a plethora of choices for your temporary home, from comfortable city hotels to quaint country guesthouses and even cozy farm stays.

The city slickers among you might prefer the hustle and bustle of Reykjavik, the capital. Here you'll find modern hotels aplenty, each more glamorous than the last. They offer all the amenities you could desire, and are within a stone's throw of the city's vibrant nightlife and cultural hotspots. However, be warned, this convenience comes at a cost. Reykjavik can be a pricey place to stay, but fear not, dear reader, for I have a solution!

For those of you with a taste for the rustic, the countryside is your oyster. Here you'll find charming guesthouses and B&B's, each with its own unique Icelandic charm. You might even share your breakfast with a friendly sheep or two. These accommodations are often family-run, offering a personal touch and a cozy atmosphere. Plus, the view of the stars at night, unobstructed by city lights, is worth every penny.

And then, for the truly adventurous, why not try a farm stay? Yes, you heard me right, a farm stay. Here, you can live like an Icelander, helping with the daily tasks and learning about their way of life. It's a unique experience, and I guarantee you'll leave with stories to tell.

But how to choose between these options? Well, my dear reader, that depends on what you're looking for. If it's nightlife and culture you're after, then Reykjavik is your best bet. If you're in need of peace and tranquillity, the countryside is calling your name. And if you want a truly unique Icelandic experience, then a farm stay is the way to go.

And then, of course, there's the question of budget. Reykjavik, as I mentioned, can be quite expensive. The countryside and farm stays, on the other hand, are often more affordable. But remember, cheap doesn't always mean bad. In fact, some of the best experiences I've had in Iceland have been in the most unexpected places.

1 Determine Your Itinerary:
- **Proximity to Attractions:** Choose accommodations that minimize travel time to the places you most want to visit. For example, if you plan to explore the Golden Circle, staying in or near Reykjavik is practical, as it serves as a convenient starting point.
- **Nature vs. City:** Decide if you prefer the urban environment of Reykjavik, with its nightlife, restaurants, and cultural scenes, or the tranquility of rural areas where natural attractions are right at your doorstep.

2 Consider Your Budget:
- **Accommodation Types:** Iceland offers a range of options from luxury hotels and boutique guesthouses to budget hostels and camping sites. Your budget will largely dictate the type of accommodation you choose.
- **Cost-Saving Tips:** Booking well in advance can secure better rates. Consider staying in guesthouses or B&Bs where you can cook some meals to save on dining out.

3 Understand Seasonal Variations:
- **Peak Season:** Accommodations in tourist-heavy areas like Reykjavik and Akureyri can fill up quickly in the summer months (June to August). Prices also peak during this time.
- **Off-Season Benefits:** Traveling in the shoulder seasons (late spring or early autumn) can offer the advantage of lower prices and fewer crowds. Winter offers unique experiences like the Northern Lights but requires staying in places that offer good access to clear skies.

4 Type of Experience:
- **Hotels and Guesthouses:** Ideal for those who appreciate comfort and convenient services like daily housekeeping and in-house dining.
- **Vacation Rentals:** Suitable for families or groups needing more space and kitchen facilities. They offer a more localized experience.
- **Hostels:** A budget-friendly option, perfect for solo travelers and young tourists. They also offer a social atmosphere to meet other travelers.
- **Farm Stays and Rural Cottages:** These provide a unique insight into

Accommodations

Icelandic rural life and are often situated in scenic locations, ideal for nature lovers.

5 Read Reviews:

• **Customer Feedback:** Check online review platforms to gauge the quality of accommodations. Reviews can provide insights into the cleanliness, service quality, and actual experiences of previous guests.

6 Accessibility and Convenience:

• **Transport Links:** If you're not renting a car, consider the availability of public transport. Some rural areas may be difficult to reach without a personal vehicle.

• **Amenities:** Ensure that your chosen accommodation provides the amenities you need, such as free Wi-Fi, parking, or accessibility features if required.

7 Local Regulations and Environment:

• **Sustainable Staying:** Opt for eco-friendly accommodations that employ sustainable practices like waste recycling, energy conservation, and support for local communities.

Booking Tips

First off, don't let them fool you into thinking that you need to book everything six months in advance. It's not like the whole world is rushing to visit Iceland, though I can't fathom why not. It's a splendid place, really. The Northern Lights alone are worth the price of admission. But I digress. While it's true that some popular spots may require a bit of advanced planning, many places are just as happy to see you show up on a whim, as long as you've got a fistful of Icelandic króna.

Now, when it comes to booking accommodations, don't be too hasty to choose the first igloo that pops up on your screen. Do a bit of digging. You'll find that there are quite a few charming options available that don't involve sleeping on a bed of ice. Consider the quaint guesthouses and cozy farm stays that offer a more authentic Icelandic experience. And don't be surprised if the owner of the place offers you a shot of Brennivín, a local spirit fondly referred to as 'Black Death'. It's all part of the hospitality, you see.

As for transportation, forget the idea of hitching a ride on a Viking longboat. Those were retired centuries ago. Your best bet is to hire a car, especially if you plan on exploring the more remote corners of the island. But heed my warning, don't get too adventurous and attempt to drive across a glacier in a compact car. That's a quick ticket to a chilly bath, and believe me, the Icelandic Search and Rescue teams have better things to do.

If you're not keen on driving, the public bus system should serve you well. Just remember to check the schedules. The buses in Iceland operate on what I like to call 'Icelandic time', which is similar to regular time, but with a lot more shrugs and a casual disregard for punctuality.

1. Leverage Local Icelandic Booking Sites:

• Instead of relying solely on international platforms, use Icelandic websites like Bungalo (for cottages), Farm Holidays (for farm stays), and Guide to Iceland (for local tours and accommodations). These sites often offer unique accommodations and experiences not listed on global platforms.

2. Consider Multi-Destination Stays:

• Iceland's diverse landscapes vary drastically from one region to another. Plan to stay in multiple locations to reduce daily travel time and immerse yourself in different environments. For example, base yourself in Vik for exploring the South Coast, Akureyri for the North, and Stykkishólmur for Snaefellsnes Peninsula adventures.

3. Utilize Iceland's Official Tourism Website for Authentic Experiences:

• Visit the official Visit Iceland website to find accredited and sustainable options that might not be heavily advertised elsewhere. This can also connect you to seasonal promotions and safety advisories directly relevant to your travel dates.

4. Tap Into Local Advice:

• Join Iceland-specific forums on TripAdvisor or Facebook groups like "Iceland Travel Advice" where locals and past travelers share up-to-date advice. This can lead to discovering hidden gems and logistical tips that enhance your experience.

5. Check for Accessibility and Inclusivity:

• If you or someone in your party has specific needs, it's crucial to confirm accessibility features with accommodations and transport providers. Not all areas are easily accessible, so this can significantly impact your planning.

6. Watch for Geothermal Hotspots:

• Accommodations close to natural hot springs can offer a memorable and uniquely Icelandic experience. Locations like the Myvatn area or those near the Secret Lagoon can provide this luxury.

7. Adjust Plans Based on Photographic Goals:

• If photography is a key part of your trip, consider the orientation of lodgings relative to key sights. For example, staying on the eastern side of major attractions can provide better sunrise photo opportunities.

8. Know Before You Go: Seasonal Road Access:

• Especially when booking for travel outside the summer season, verify that the attractions you plan to visit are accessible. Roads like those to Landmannalaugar are only open in the summer, which could affect where you decide to stay in spring or fall.

9. Early Bird or Last Minute?

Accommodations

- While generally booking early is advised, last-minute bookings can some-times yield unexpected deals, especially for day tours and excursions which might offer discounted rates to fill spots.

10. Integrate Tech Tools:

- Use apps like Aurora Forecast for Northern Lights planning or Vegagerdin for real-time road conditions to align your stay locations with the activities and expe-riences you prioritize each day.

Recommendations By Region

In the south, the land of waterfalls and geysers, the lamb is king. The sheep here graze freely on the hillsides, munching on a diet of wild herbs and berries, and the resulting meat is a succulent treat that will send your taste buds into a frenzy of delight. Try the smoked lamb, or hangikjöt, a traditional dish usually served at Christmas but available year-round for those who know where to look.

The west is home to the snæfellsnes peninsula, a place so magical it inspired Jules Verne's 'Journey to the Center of the Earth'. Here, the seafood is the star of the show. The cold, clean waters yield a bounty of fish and shellfish, all of which are hauled in fresh each morning. Seek out a bowl of hearty fish soup, or plokkfiskur, a comforting stew made with potatoes and white fish.

As you venture north, into the land of the midnight sun, you'll find a region where the volcanic soil produces a rich bounty of root vegetables. The potatoes, carrots, and turnips grown here are unlike any you've tasted before, and they form the backbone of many a hearty, warming dish. Do try the rúgbrauð, a type of rye bread that's traditionally baked in the ground using geothermal heat.

Finally, in the southwest, you'll find Reykjavik, a city that's as cosmopolitan as it is charming. Here, you'll find every type of cuisine under the sun, from tradi-tional Icelandic fare to international fusion. Don't miss out on trying the hot dogs from Bæjarins Beztu Pylsur, a humble food stand that's been serving up the best hot dogs in the world since 1937.

Each region of Iceland has its own culinary traditions, shaped by the unique landscapes and climates of this beautiful, rugged country. So, as you travel, don't just feast your eyes on the stunning vistas - feast your taste buds on the delicious, hearty fare that's waiting for you in every corner of this frosty paradise.

Eastern Iceland:

In the east, home to dramatic fjords and extensive forests, the cuisine features both land and sea. Wild game, particularly reindeer, is a highlight in this region. The animals graze in the wild highlands, making their meat exceptionally flavorful and lean. Local restaurants often serve reindeer steak or stew, seasoned with local herbs and berries. Seafood, too, remains a staple, with dishes frequently featuring fresh haddock or langoustine, celebrated for their sweetness and texture.

For a truly local experience, seek out a dish of *Svið*, a traditional Icelandic meal made from singed and boiled sheep's head, which is available in specialty eateries throughout the region. Pair this with a side of *kartöflumús* (mashed potatoes) or fresh local vegetables for a hearty meal.

Traditional Beverages:

No gastronomic tour is complete without sampling the local beverages. In Iceland, this means tasting the *Brennivín*, also known as Black Death—a potent schnapps made from fermented potato mash and flavored with caraway. For those preferring something a bit milder, Icelandic craft beers are on the rise, with local breweries in Reykjavik and Akureyri offering a range of styles from pale ales to volcanic stouts, each incorporating local ingredients like Arctic berries, Icelandic barley, and glacial water.

Local Festivals:

To truly immerse yourself in Iceland's food culture, plan your visit around local food festivals. The Great Fish Day in Dalvík, held every August, is where the entire town comes together to cook and serve fish dishes to visitors for free. Another must-visit is the Reykjavik Food and Fun Festival in March, which combines the culinary skills of international chefs with the best of Icelandic ingredients.

Foraging and Sustainability:

Iceland's unique environment lends itself to foraging, a practice many local chefs incorporate into their menus. From berries and mushrooms in the late summer to seaweed along the coastline, foraging provides a connection to the land that translates directly into the cuisine. This practice not only supports sustainability but also encourages you to explore and taste the landscape in its purest form.

Culinary Souvenirs:

Before departing this enchanting island, consider taking home culinary souvenirs. Options abound from smoked lamb, Icelandic sea salt—a favorite among chefs for its texture and purity—to hand-harvested Arctic thyme or birch syrup. Each embodies the flavors of Iceland and provides a tasty reminder of your journey.

Iceland's Regions At A Glance

Now, I reckon it's about time we took a gander at the various regions of this frosty wonderland they call Iceland. Not to be confused with the supermarket, of course. That's a completely different kind of frozen.

First off, we've got the Capital Region. This is where you'll find Reykjavik, the beating heart of Iceland. It's the biggest city in the country, though that's a bit like being the tallest dwarf. It's filled with all sorts of modern amenities, like buildings and such. The nightlife is said to be quite vibrant, if you don't mind the occasional volcanic eruption livening up your evening.

Next, we have the West. This is where you'll find the Snæfellsnes Peninsula, home to Snæfellsjökull National Park. Now, I know what you're thinking. "That sounds like a sneeze!" And you'd be right. But it's also a majestic glacier-capped volcano, so let's not get too hung up on the name, shall we?

The East, on the other hand, is a haven for wildlife lovers. Here you can find the largest reindeer herd in Iceland. Just remember, these ain't your Christmas card reindeer. They're wild, rugged, and won't hesitate to charge if they think you're after their carrots.

The North is known for its breathtaking landscapes, including the mighty Dettifoss waterfall. Standing at the edge of this behemoth, you can't help but feel a sense of awe... and a strong desire not to slip. It's also home to the town of Akureyri, or as I like to call it, "Reykjavik's less popular sibling."

The South, meanwhile, is home to the famous Golden Circle. This is a popular tourist route that includes the geysers of Geysir, the waterfall of Gullfoss, and the national park of Þingvellir. I'm told it's quite the sight, assuming you can pronounce any of it.

Finally, we have the Highlands, a vast, uninhabited area in the center of the country. It's a harsh, desolate landscape, much like my Aunt Mabel's fruitcake. But it's also stunningly beautiful, in a rugged, untamed sort of way. Just remember to pack warm clothes. And maybe a flare gun.

Well, there you have it, a whirlwind tour of Iceland's regions. Each one is unique, with its own character and charm. And they're all colder than a penguin's picnic. But that's part of the appeal, right? After all, if you wanted sun and sand, you'd go to the Bahamas. But where's the adventure in that?

Capital Region:

Centered around Reykjavik, the Capital Region is not only the administrative heart but also the cultural pulse of Iceland. Here, the blend of Scandinavian architectural charm and vibrant street art tells the modern tale of a city that treasures its historical roots. Reykjavik is compact yet cosmopolitan, hosting an array of museums, galleries, and theaters, alongside an eclectic food scene that spans traditional Icelandic cuisines to global gourmet offerings. The city is also the launching point for  various excursions into the natural wonders of Iceland, making it a versatile base for both urban and adventure tourism.

West Iceland:

The West is characterized by its diverse landscapes, from the lava fields and hot springs to the lush valleys dotted with historical sites. The Snæfellsnes Peninsula, often called 'Iceland in Miniature,' encapsulates this diversity with its dramatic Snæfellsjökull glacier, rugged coastlines, and charming fishing villages. This region is steeped in folklore and history, with ancient saga sites and tales of elves and trolls that captivate visitors' imaginations.

Accommodations

East Iceland:

Known for its serene fjords, the East boasts some of Iceland's most untamed landscapes. It's less traversed by tourists, offering a peaceful retreat with breathtaking views and abundant wildlife, including the largest reindeer herd in the country. The region is also celebrated for its arts and crafts, particularly in Seydisfjordur, a quaint town known for its vibrant arts scene and the annual LungA Art Festival.

North Iceland:

The North of Iceland is home to some of the country's most iconic natural attractions, including Lake Mývatn with its unique volcanic formations and rich birdlife, and Dettifoss, the most powerful waterfall in Europe. Akureyri, the 'Capital of the North,' serves as a cultural and economic hub in the region and is known for its botanical gardens and vibrant arts scene. The area is also a prime location for witnessing the Northern Lights during the winter months.

South Iceland:

The South is perhaps the most visited region due to the Golden Circle route, featuring Þingvellir National Park, the Gullfoss waterfall, and the Geysir geothermal area. Beyond these iconic sites, the South is also home to the impressive Seljalandsfoss and Skógafoss waterfalls and the black sand beaches of Vik. Its proximity to the capital makes it a popular choice for both short visits and longer explorations.

Near Keflavík International Airport (KEF)
1 Hotel Berg

- **Location**: Bakkavegur 17, Keflavík
- **Highlights**: Overlooks the marina, offers a rooftop pool, and is just a 10-minute drive from the airport.
- **Things to Visit**: The Viking World Museum and Reykjanes Art Museum.
- **Top Restaurant**: Kaffi Duus – known for its seafood, located at Duusgata 10.

2 Park Inn by Radisson Reykjavik Keflavik Airport

- **Location**: Hafnargata 57, Keflavík
- **Highlights**: Offers spacious rooms and a convenient location close to the airport and Blue Lagoon.
- **Things to Visit**: Blue Lagoon is just a 20-minute drive away.
- **Top Restaurant**: Rain – specializes in fusion dishes, located at Hafnargata 19.

Near Reykjavík Airport (RKV)
1 Reykjavik Residence Hotel

- **Location**: Hverfisgata 45, Reykjavík
- **Highlights**: Boutique apartments in the heart of the city with easy access to downtown attractions.

- **Things to Visit**: Hallgrímskirkja and the National Museum of Iceland.
- **Top Restaurant**: Dill Restaurant – New Nordic cuisine, located at Hverfisgata 12.

2 Icelandair Hotel Reykjavik Marina
- **Location**: Mýrargata 2, Reykjavík
- **Highlights**: Stylish waterfront hotel near the city center with a vibrant atmosphere.
- **Things to Visit**: Harpa Concert Hall and Reykjavik Old Harbour.
- **Top Restaurant**: Slippbarinn – offers creative cocktails and local dishes, located within the hotel.

Near Akureyri Airport (AEY)

1 Hotel Kea by Keahotels
- **Location**: Hafnarstræti 87-89, Akureyri
- **Highlights**: Located in the heart of Akureyri with views of the fjord and mountains.
- **Things to Visit**: Akureyri Church and Akureyri Botanical Garden.
- **Top Restaurant**: Bautinn – a local favorite for traditional Icelandic dishes, located at Hafnarstræti 92.

2 Icelandair Hotel Akureyri
- **Location**: Þingvallastræti 23, Akureyri
- **Highlights**: A modern hotel set in a beautiful location near the Botanical Gardens.
- **Things to Visit**: The Arctic Botanical Gardens (Lystigarðurinn) and Akureyri Art Museum.
- **Top Restaurant**: Strikið – offers stunning views and a mix of Icelandic and international cuisine, located at Skipagata 14.

Chapter 6
Discovering Iceland

OVERVIEW OF EACH REGION

Let's start with the capital, Reykjavik. Now, this city is a bit like a rebellious teenager; it's modern, it's vibrant, and it's got a bit of an attitude. It's a city that's constantly on the move, constantly evolving. You can spend your days exploring the colorful streets, taking in the contemporary architecture, and sampling the local cuisine. Oh, and speaking of cuisine, if you're brave enough, you might want to try hákarl. It's fermented shark and let me tell you, it's an experience.

Next up, we have the Westfjords. This is a place where nature takes center stage. It's a land of towering cliffs, cascading waterfalls, and quaint fishing villages. If the city life in Reykjavik is a bit too much for you, the Westfjords is the perfect antidote. There's a tranquility here that's hard to find elsewhere. But don't let the serenity fool you; the Westfjords has its own brand of excitement. There's the annual bird-watching festival, for instance. Yes, bird-watching. Don't knock it until you've tried it.

We then move on to the South Coast. Now, this is where things get a bit dramatic. The South Coast is home to some of Iceland's most iconic landscapes.

There's the black sand beach of Vik, the Jökulsárlón glacier lagoon, and the Selja-landsfoss waterfall. It's a place that's both beautiful and a little intimidating. It's like the popular girl in high school; you can't help but admire her, but you're also a bit scared of her.

Next, we head to the North. This is a place of extremes. In the summer, the sun barely sets, and in the winter, the Northern Lights put on a show that's nothing short of magical. The North is also home to Lake Mývatn, a place that's both serene and surreal. It's a bit like stepping into a dream. A dream with a lot of mosquitoes, mind you, but a dream nonetheless.

Finally, we have the East. This is a place that's often overlooked by tourists, and frankly, I think that's a shame. The East is home to some of the most stunning fjords in the country, not to mention a number of charming small towns. It's a place where you can truly get away from it all.

Top Attractions

My dear reader, I have been led to believe that you are a person of considerable taste, a true connoisseur of the extraordinary and the breathtaking. If that be the case, then you, my friend, are in for a treat. Iceland, this ethereal land of fire and ice, is generously endowed with natural spectacles that can make even the most seasoned of travelers go weak in the knees.

Now, I'm going to let you in on a little secret. The Blue Lagoon, with its milky blue, geothermal waters, is not just a sight for sore eyes; it's also a balm for weary spirits. This is a place where you can soak in the warmth, literally and metaphorically, while the icy winds play a symphony in the background. The occasional sight of an aurora borealis painting the sky in surreal hues is merely an added bonus, a cherry on top if you will.

But wait, there's more! The Golden Circle, a 300-kilometer loop from Reykjavik into the southern uplands and back, is like a 'greatest hits' collection of Iceland's natural wonders. There's the Gullfoss waterfall, where the water seems to plunge into the earth's core. Watching it feels like a thrilling roller coaster ride, only without the safety harness. Then there's the Geysir geothermal area, a veritable pressure cooker of the earth, where hot springs bubble and geysers erupt with a hiss and a roar, much to the delight of onlookers.

Now, if you're a fan of Jules Verne's 'Journey to the Center of the Earth', you might want to pay a visit to the Snæfellsjökull glacier. This majestic glacier-capped stratovolcano, located on the Snæfellsnes peninsula, was the supposed entrance to the earth's core in Verne's novel. While I can't guarantee a journey to the earth's center, I can promise you an unforgettable hike and some truly spectacular views.

And speaking of spectacular views, the Vatnajökull National Park is another must-see. Spanning a whopping 14% of the country's land area, it's home to the largest glacier in Europe, the highest mountain in Iceland, and some of the most active volcanoes. It's like Mother Nature decided to show off all her best assets in one place!

If you're more of a city slicker, don't worry, Iceland's got you covered too. Reykjavik, the world's northernmost capital, is a charming blend of old and new. From the striking concrete Hallgrímskirkja church and the revolving Perlan glass dome offering panoramic views of the city, to the vibrant street art and cozy cafés, Reykjavik is a feast for the senses.

The Northern Lights:

For many, the celestial dance of the Aurora Borealis is a bucket-list spectacle. The best places in Iceland to witness this natural wonder include the dark, clear skies above Þingvellir National Park or from the comfort of a geothermal hot tub in one of the remote countryside hotels in the North. The lights are most visible from September to April, and their ethereal glow will leave you awestruck.

Diamond Beach:

On the South Coast near Jökulsárlón Glacier Lagoon, you'll find Diamond Beach, a striking black volcanic sand beach where icebergs from the lagoon wash ashore and glitter like diamonds on the dark sand. Watching these translucent ice chunks contrast with the black sand and listening to the ocean waves is a surreal experience, showcasing nature's artistry.

The East Fjords:
Less frequented by tourists, the East Fjords are a serene collection of majestic fjords, rugged cliffs, and quaint fishing villages. This region offers a peaceful escape with breathtaking scenic drives and an abundance of wildlife, including puffins and reindeer. The charming village of Seyðisfjörður, with its colorful wooden houses and artistic community, is a highlight.

Askja Caldera:
For those willing to venture into the central highlands, the lunar landscapes surrounding Askja Caldera are otherworldly. A hike to the Viti explosion crater, filled with geothermally heated water, offers a unique bathing experience in the middle of volcanic terrain. This area's stark beauty offers a profound sense of isolation and tranquility.

The Westman Islands:
Located off the South Coast, this archipelago is known for its volcanic activity and rich birdlife, including the world's largest puffin colony. A visit to Heimaey, the only inhabited island, provides insights into Icelandic resilience and ingenuity, particularly the efforts to save the town from a devastating 1973 volcanic eruption by pumping seawater onto the advancing lava.

Skógafoss and Seljalandsfoss Waterfalls:
These waterfalls epitomize the dramatic beauty of Iceland's landscape. Skógafoss, one of the biggest waterfalls in the country, offers a picturesque view of water cascading down 60 meters over a cliff. Nearby, Seljalandsfoss features a unique path that allows visitors to walk behind the waterfall's veil, offering a unique perspective and stunning photo opportunities.

Cultural Festivals:
Iceland's vibrant cultural scene is best experienced through its festivals. Whether it's the lively atmosphere of Reykjavik Pride, the cultural immersion of the Secret Solstice Festival celebrating the midnight sun, or the traditional Viking Festival in Hafnarfjörður, these events are perfect for experiencing Iceland's modern culture and historical heritage.

Hidden Gems

You can't talk about Iceland without mentioning its underground food scene. No, I don't mean food grown underground, though with the geothermal energy here, I wouldn't be surprised. I'm talking about the food market of Hlemmur Mathöll. It's a haven for food enthusiasts, offering a range of cuisines from Vietnamese street food to Nordic sushi. It's a place where locals and tourists collide in a delicious melting pot of cultures and flavors.

Now, if you've got a taste for the unusual, the fermented shark, or hákarl, is a must-try. I'll admit, I've had socks that smelled better, but hey, when in Iceland, right? If that's too adventurous for you, there's always the Icelandic hot dog, or pylsa. It's not your average hot dog, mind you. It's served with a mix of raw and fried onions, ketchup, sweet mustard, and remoulade. It might sound like a strange combination, but trust me, it's a taste sensation.

Moving on from the culinary delights, let's talk about the natural wonders. Now, everyone's heard of the geysers and glaciers, but have you heard of the Inside the Volcano tour? You get to descend into the magma chamber of a dormant volcano. It's like Jules Verne's 'Journey to the Center of the Earth', but without the dinosaurs and giant mushrooms. It's a once-in-a-lifetime experience, and I can assure you, it's worth every penny.

If you prefer your adventures on the cooler side, the ice caves of Vatnajökull glacier are a sight to behold. The blue ice, the shimmering lights, it's like stepping into another world. But remember to wrap up warm, it can get a bit nippy.

As for the history buffs, the Settlement Exhibition in Reykjavik offers a glimpse into the Viking Age. It's an interactive museum built around a 10th-century long-house. It's a bit like a time machine, only without the flux capacitor.

For those who enjoy a good soak, the Secret Lagoon in Fludir is a must-visit. It's less crowded than the Blue Lagoon but just as relaxing. Plus, you get to enjoy the northern lights without the touristy hustle and bustle.

Criteria for Selection:

• **Uniqueness:** Each location offers something not found elsewhere or provides an unusual experience.

• **Tourist Traffic:** These spots attract fewer tourists, offering a more serene and intimate experience.

• **Cultural or Historical Significance:** Places that hold significance locally or tell a story about Iceland's heritage and traditions.

List of Hidden Gems Organized Geographically

North Iceland:

• **Hvítserkur**

• **Location:** Vatnsnes Peninsula, Coordinates: 65.6066° N, 20.6357° W

• **Description:** Hvítserkur is a striking 15-meter high basalt stack resembling a dragon drinking from the water. Local legends speak of this rock as a petrified troll.

• **Photographs:** [Include Images]

• **Best Time to Visit:** Early morning for sunrise, which illuminates the rock beautifully and enhances photography opportunities.

• **Accessibility:** Accessible by a short hike from the nearest parking area; paths can be slippery.

• **Local Tips:** Check the tide times to see Hvítserkur reflected in the water. Nearby, the coastal area is great for spotting seals.

• **Safety Considerations:** Wear sturdy shoes as the path to the viewpoint can be rocky and wet.

East Iceland:

• **Stuðlagil Canyon**

• **Location:** Near Jökuldalur Valley, Coordinates: 65.0732° N, 15.8769° W

• **Description:** This canyon, characterized by its stunning basalt columns and one of the largest collections in Iceland, was hidden beneath a river until a dam reduced the water levels.

- **Photographs:** [Include Images]
- **Best Time to Visit:** Late spring to early autumn when the river is calm and the basalt columns are fully visible.
- **Accessibility:** Requires a hike which can be moderately challenging.
- **Local Tips:** For the best photographic light, visit during midday when the sun illuminates the entire canyon.
- **Safety Considerations:** The path may be muddy and slippery; appropriate footwear is essential.

South Iceland:
- **Rauðfeldsgjá Gorge**
- **Location:** Snaefellsnes Peninsula, Coordinates: 64.8096° N, 23.7142° W
- **Description:** A deep gorge that cuts into the mountain, offering an adventurous climb and stunning views from within.
- **Photographs:** [Include Images]
- **Best Time to Visit:** Summer for easier access and safer climbing conditions.
- **Accessibility:** The initial part of the hike is accessible to most, but the inner parts require climbing and are more suited to those in good physical condition.
- **Local Tips:** Wear waterproof clothing as you may need to wade through water.
- **Safety Considerations:** Not recommended in wet conditions as the rocks become very slippery.

West Iceland:
- **Glymur Waterfall**
- **Location:** Hvalfjörður Fjord, Coordinates: 64.3837° N, 21.2002° W
- **Description:** The second-highest waterfall in Iceland, Glymur is surrounded by lush vegetation and dramatic cliffs, offering a rewarding hike.
- **Photographs:** [Include Images]
- **Best Time to Visit:** Late spring through early autumn when the trail is most accessible.
- **Accessibility:** The hike to Glymur involves river crossings, steep climbs, and requires good physical condition.
- **Local Tips:** Bring a camera with a good zoom to capture the waterfall from various angles.
- **Safety Considerations:** The river crossing can be dangerous, especially if the water level is high.

Adventures And Activities

First off, there's the thrill of whale watching. I'm not talking about little guppies here, but massive, awe-inspiring creatures that leap from the water with a grace that belies their size. You can find yourself a boat tour right out of Reykjavik harbor, and I promise you, the sight of these majestic beasts will leave you speechless.

Then there's the spectacle of the Northern Lights. Now, I don't care how many pictures you've seen, nothing, and I mean nothing, can prepare you for the real deal. It's like nature decided to put on a light show just for you. If you're lucky enough to be visiting between September and April, make sure you find a dark, clear night, look up and wait for the magic to happen.

For those of you with a taste for the extreme, why not try your hand at glacier hiking? That's right, you can walk on a glacier. With a guide, of course. The ice is slicker than a politician's speech, and you don't want to end up sliding down a crevasse. But once you get the hang of it, the view from the top is worth every bit of the effort.

If you're more of a water baby, a dip in the geothermal pools is a must. Picture this: It's freezing outside, but you're soaking in a naturally heated pool, surrounded by snow-covered mountains. It's like a hot tub, but better, because it's Mother Nature's hot tub.

But wait, there's more! You can go horse riding on Icelandic horses, those sturdy, friendly creatures that are as much a part of the landscape as the mountains and the sea. Or you can explore the black sand beaches, a stark and beautiful contrast to the white snow. And don't forget about the ice caves, the waterfalls, the puffin colonies... the list goes on.

And when you're done with the day's adventures, you can head back to town, find a cozy restaurant, and dig into some hearty Icelandic food. You've earned it, after all.

Categorization of Activities:

1 Water Sports:

• **Kayaking and Canoeing:**

• **Name:** Glacier Lagoon Kayaking

• **Description:** Paddle through the serene waters of Jökulsárlón Glacier Lagoon, navigating between icebergs of all shapes and sizes, with breathtaking views of the glacier.

• **Location and Accessibility:** Jökulsárlón, Southeast Iceland, accessible by car from Reykjavik (about 5 hours drive).

• **Duration and Timing:** 2-3 hours, best from May to September.

- **Cost and Booking:** Approximately $100 per person; advance booking recommended.
- **Equipment and Preparation:** Kayaks and safety gear provided; dress in warm, waterproof clothing.
- **Difficulty Level:** Beginner to intermediate; no prior kayaking experience needed.
- **Safety Measures:** Guided by professionals; includes a safety briefing.

2 Hiking and Trekking:

- **Name:** Hiking the Laugavegur Trail
- **Description:** Trek through diverse and spectacular landscapes, from colorful rhyolite mountains and geothermal areas to vast black sand deserts and deep forests.
- **Location and Accessibility:** Begins at Landmannalaugar, accessible by mountain bus from Reykjavik during the summer months.
- **Duration and Timing:** 4-5 days, best from late June to September.
- **Cost and Booking:** Free to hike; hut fees apply for overnight stays, and reservations are necessary.
- **Equipment and Preparation:** Hikers need to bring their own gear and supplies; preparation for changeable weather is crucial.
- **Difficulty Level:** Intermediate to advanced.
- **Safety Measures:** Weather can change rapidly; GPS and map required.

3 Cultural Tours:

- **Name:** Reykjavik City Walking Tour
- **Description:** Explore the culture, history, and architecture of Iceland's capital with a knowledgeable local guide.
- **Location and Accessibility:** Downtown Reykjavik, easily accessible on foot.
- **Duration and Timing:** 2-3 hours, available year-round.
- **Cost and Booking:** Approximately $30-50 per person; booking in advance is recommended but not necessary.
- **Equipment and Preparation:** Comfortable walking shoes and suitable clothing for the weather.
- **Difficulty Level:** Easy.
- **Safety Measures:** Urban environment; low risk.

4 Wildlife Encounters:

- **Name:** Whale Watching in Husavik
- **Description:** Husavik is known as the whale watching capital of Iceland, with frequent sightings of humpback and minke whales.
- **Location and Accessibility:** Husavik, North Iceland, accessible by car or bus from Reykjavik.
- **Duration and Timing:** About 3 hours, best from April to October.

- **Cost and Booking:** Around $80-$100 per person; advance booking advised.
- **Equipment and Preparation:** Warm and waterproof clothing recommended; binoculars provided.
- **Difficulty Level:** Easy.
- **Safety Measures:** Life jackets provided; boats are equipped for safety and comfort.

5 Ice Caving:

- **Name:** Vatnajökull Ice Cave Exploration
- **Description:** Venture into the mesmerizing blue ice caves beneath Europe's largest glacier, Vatnajökull, for a once-in-a-lifetime exploration of stunning ice formations.
- **Location and Accessibility:** Vatnajökull National Park, Southeast Iceland, accessible via guided tours from nearby towns like Skaftafell.
- **Duration and Timing:** About 2-4 hours, best from November to March when the ice is most stable.
- **Cost and Booking:** Around $150-$200 per person; mandatory advance booking as tours are led by certified glacier guides.
- **Equipment and Preparation:** Helmets, ice axes, and crampons provided; wear warm, waterproof clothing.
- **Difficulty Level:** Moderate; requires walking on ice, often in cold conditions.
- **Safety Measures:** Led by experienced guides; safety gear provided.

6 Off-road Jeep Tours:

- **Name:** Thorsmork Valley Super Jeep Adventure
- **Description:** Traverse rough terrains and cross glacial rivers in a super jeep to reach the stunning Thorsmork Valley, surrounded by majestic mountains and glaciers.
- **Location and Accessibility:** Thorsmork Valley, accessible only by 4x4 vehicles capable of river crossings, tours depart from Reykjavik or Hvolsvöllur.
- **Duration and Timing:** Full-day adventure, best from May to September.
- **Cost and Booking:** Approximately $200-$300 per person; booking in advance is necessary.
- **Equipment and Preparation:** Dress in layers suitable for changing weather conditions; bring snacks and water.
- **Difficulty Level:** Easy to moderate; the tour itself is not physically demanding, but involves rough riding.
- **Safety Measures:** Experienced drivers navigate challenging conditions; passengers should be prepared for bumpy rides.

7 Northern Lights Hunting:

- **Name:** Aurora Borealis Night Tour

- **Description:** Chase the Northern Lights with expert guides who use local weather knowledge to find the best viewing spots away from light pollution.
- **Location and Accessibility:** Tours typically depart from Reykjavik and venture into rural areas optimal for sightings.
- **Duration and Timing:** Approximately 3-5 hours, best from September to April.
- **Cost and Booking:** About $50-$100 per person; dependent on weather conditions, so booking with a flexible cancellation policy is advised.
- **Equipment and Preparation:** Warm clothing and patience are essential; camera with manual settings recommended for photography.
- **Difficulty Level:** Easy; involves nighttime travel and waiting outdoors in cold conditions.
- **Safety Measures:** Tours are weather-dependent with flexibility for rescheduling; guides ensure safety in remote areas.

8 Snorkeling and Diving:

- **Name:** Silfra Fissure Snorkeling
- **Description:** Snorkel between the tectonic plates of North America and Eurasia in the crystal-clear waters of Silfra Fissure, known for its incredible underwater visibility.
- **Location and Accessibility:** Thingvellir National Park, about an hour's drive from Reykjavik.
- **Duration and Timing:** About 2-3 hours in the water; available year-round, though water temperatures are consistently cold.
- **Cost and Booking:** Around $140-$180 per person; includes all necessary snorkeling gear, must be booked in advance.
- **Equipment and Preparation:** Dry suits and snorkeling equipment provided; participants should be comfortable swimming in cold water.
- **Difficulty Level:** Moderate; requires good physical health and comfort with cold water.
- **Safety Measures:** Professional guides accompany all tours, and safety briefings on hypothermia and equipment use are provided.

9 Horseback Riding:

- **Name:** Icelandic Horse Riding Tour
- **Description:** Experience Iceland's landscapes on the back of an Icelandic horse, known for its unique tölt gait, offering a smooth ride through lava fields and alongside mountain trails.
- **Location and Accessibility:** Various locations, including just outside Reykjavik and in more remote countryside areas.
- **Duration and Timing:** Tours range from 1 hour to full-day excursions; available year-round.

- **Cost and Booking:** Starts at around $75 per person for a shorter tour; prices vary based on duration and tour complexity.
- **Equipment and Preparation:** Helmets and riding gear provided; wear comfortable clothing and sturdy shoes.
- **Difficulty Level:** Beginner to advanced; no previous riding experience required for many tours.
- **Safety Measures:** All riders are given a safety briefing, and rides are matched to rider skill level.

Chapter 7
Experiences and Adventures

OUTDOOR ADVENTURES (HIKING, BIKING, WILDLIFE WATCHING)

In the land of fire and ice, one might expect to find dragons, not unlike those in the tales of yore. But fear not, dear traveler! The dragons of Iceland are of a different breed altogether. They are the towering mountains, the thundering waterfalls, the creeping glaciers, and the whispering winds. And what better way to commune with these ancient 'dragons' than to lace up your boots, hop on a bike, or train your binoculars on the local wildlife?

Now, I can see you there, scratching your head and saying, "Mr. Twain, I am not the adventurous sort. I prefer a good book and a warm fire to braving the elements." To which I say, "Nonsense! You have the spirit of an explorer within you, I am sure of it! Why else would you have picked up this guide to Iceland, a land as wild and untamed as a young colt?"

Let's start with hiking, shall we? Iceland's trails are not for the faint-hearted. They wind through rugged terrain, along cliff edges, up steep inclines, and through fields of lava rock as sharp as a barber's razor. But oh, the rewards! To stand atop a mountain peak, the wind whipping at your coat, the view stretching out before you like a painting, is a feeling akin to flying.

Iceland's trails are like a buffet for the senses. There are the vibrant greens of moss-covered rocks, the icy blues of glacier lagoons, the stark blacks of volcanic beaches, and the fiery reds of sunsets that seem to set the whole world ablaze. And the smells! There's the fresh, clean scent of the air, the earthy aroma of the soil, the tangy saltiness of the sea, and the occasional whiff of sulfur, a reminder of the geothermal activity simmering beneath your feet.

Now, if hiking sounds too arduous, perhaps you'd prefer to explore on two wheels? Biking allows you to cover more ground and feel the exhilaration of the wind in your hair. The roads and trails are well-maintained, and there's a certain joy in pedaling along, surrounded by nothing but nature's grandeur. Just remember to pack a hearty lunch, for biking in Iceland is sure to work up an appetite.

Hiking

1. Laugavegur Trail

- **Description:** Renowned as one of the most beautiful hiking trails in the world, the Laugavegur Trail offers a remarkable 55-kilometer trek through diverse landscapes including mountains, hot springs, rivers, and glacial valleys.
- **Location:** The trail connects Landmannalaugar in the highlands to Þórsmörk, a valley nestled at the foot of the famous Eyjafjallajökull volcano.
- **Duration and Timing:** Typically completed over 4-5 days; best hiked from June to September when the trail is most accessible.
- **Difficulty Level:** Moderate to challenging; suitable for those with some hiking experience due to varying weather conditions and terrain.
- **Equipment and Preparation:** Full hiking gear required, including waterproof clothing, good hiking boots, and camping equipment if staying in huts or camping along the route.

Biking

2. Reykjavik Coastal Path

- **Description:** A scenic route perfect for casual biking, this path stretches along the coastline offering stunning views of the sea, mountains, and cityscape of Reykjavik.
- **Location:** Starts from the Harpa Concert Hall and stretches around the Seltjarnarnes peninsula.
- **Duration and Timing:** The path is approximately 10 kilometers long and can be enjoyed in 1-2 hours, depending on stops and pace.
- **Difficulty Level:** Easy; suitable for all ages and skill levels, including families with children.
- **Equipment and Preparation:** Bikes can be rented from several locations in Reykjavik. No special gear needed aside from typical cycling attire.

Wildlife Watching

3. Whale Watching in Husavik

- **Description:** Husavik is often called the whale watching capital of Iceland. Tours offer close encounters with various species including minke, humpback, blue, and orca whales in their natural habitat.
- **Location:** Departures are from Husavik harbor, located in North Iceland.
- **Duration and Timing:** Tours typically last between 3 to 5 hours and are best from April to October when marine life is most active.
- **Difficulty Level:** Easy; suitable for all ages and fitness levels.

- **Equipment and Preparation:** Warm and waterproof clothing recommended as temperatures on the water can be much colder. Most tours provide overalls and life vests.

4. Puffin Watching on the Westman Islands

- **Description:** The Westman Islands, particularly the island of Heimaey, are home to one of the world's largest puffin colonies. The islands provide a unique opportunity to observe these charming birds up close.
- **Location:** Heimaey, the largest of the Westman Islands, accessible by ferry from Landeyjahöfn.
- **Duration and Timing:** Best visited during the nesting season from early May to August.
- **Difficulty Level:** Easy to moderate, depending on whether you choose to explore more rugged parts of the island.
- **Equipment and Preparation:** Binoculars enhance the viewing experience, and sturdy shoes are recommended for walking the island's trails.

Hiking

5. Fimmvörðuháls Pass

- **Description:** This challenging hike takes you between the Eyjafjallajökull and Mýrdalsjökull glaciers, offering spectacular views of new lava fields created by recent volcanic eruptions.
- **Location:** The trail starts at Skógar, follows up past the stunning Skógafoss waterfall, and ends in Þórsmörk.
- **Duration and Timing:** This is a 22-kilometer hike that most complete in one long day, though it can also be split over two days. Best attempted in the summer months when the path is clear of snow.
- **Difficulty Level:** Challenging; suitable for experienced hikers due to steep gradients and potentially tricky weather conditions.
- **Equipment and Preparation:** Weather-appropriate hiking gear is necessary, including layers for cold and wet conditions. Navigation tools are recommended.

Biking

6. Westfjords Way

- **Description:** Experience the remote Westfjords via this challenging cycling route that covers dramatic landscapes, from steep fjords to rugged cliffs, providing a solitary journey back in time.
- **Location:** Loop starting and ending in Ísafjörður, covering roughly 950 kilometers of challenging terrain.
- **Duration and Timing:** Ideally, this journey takes about 10-14 days, depending on pace. The best times to attempt are late spring through early fall.
- **Difficulty Level:** Advanced; due to the length and sometimes harsh weather conditions, it's recommended for experienced cyclists.

- **Equipment and Preparation:** A well-maintained mountain or hybrid bike camping gear for remote areas, and strong navigation skills are essential.

Wildlife Watching

7. Arctic Fox Watching in Hornstrandir

- **Description:** The Hornstrandir Nature Reserve is one of the best places in Iceland to watch Arctic foxes in their natural habitat. These creatures are protected here, making them less shy and more visible to visitors.
- **Location:** Accessible by boat from Ísafjörður; located in the northernmost part of the Westfjords.
- **Duration and Timing:** Day trips are possible, but staying a few days increases the chances of sightings. The best time is during the summer months when the reserve is most accessible.
- **Difficulty Level:** Moderate to challenging, depending on how much of the area you plan to explore.
- **Equipment and Preparation:** Bring binoculars for better viewing, and ensure you have waterproof and warm clothing.

8. Seal Watching at Vatnsnes Peninsula

- **Description:** The Vatnsnes Peninsula in North Iceland is an excellent spot for observing seals in their natural coastal environment. The loop road around the peninsula offers various viewpoints and a seal center that provides insights into these marine mammals.
- **Location:** An easy drive from Hvammstangi, which is about 197 kilometers from Reykjavik.
- **Duration and Timing:** The peninsula can be explored in a day; however, lingering at seal hotspots increases your chances of a sighting. Year-round visibility, but June and July are particularly good for seeing mothers with pups.
- **Difficulty Level:** Easy; accessible by car and short walks to viewing points.
- **Equipment and Preparation:** Bring a good camera with a zoom lens and binoculars for distant viewing. Dress warmly, as winds can be cold and brisk by the coast.

Thermal Pools And Spas

Iceland is dotted with these hot spots, no pun intended, and they are as much a part of the culture as the sagas, the elves, and that fermented shark dish that I still can't pronounce. These thermal pools aren't just for show, oh no. They are nature's own hot tubs, heated by the earth's very own belly, and they offer a warmth that's more than just skin deep.

Now, if you find yourself in the capital, Reykjavik, you'll want to pay a visit to the Blue Lagoon. It's a tourist hotspot, and with good reason. The waters are a milky blue, warm and inviting, and the steam rising from the surface gives the place an otherworldly feel. It's like bathing in a dream, or a cloud, or a cloud's dream. And the silica mud they give you to smear on your face? Why, it'll make your skin smoother than a politician's promises.

But, if you're more of a backroads traveler, preferring the path less trodden, then you might fancy a dip in one of the country's many natural hot springs. These are scattered all over the island, like nature's own little surprises, and they are as varied as the Icelandic weather. Some are tucked away in lava fields, others peek out from under snowy mountains, and a few are so remote that you'll need a horse, a compass, and a good dose of courage to find them.

One such hidden gem is the Landmannalaugar geothermal area. It's a bit of a trek to get there, but once you do, you'll be rewarded with a natural hot spring that's tucked away in the highlands. The water is warm, the scenery is breathtaking, and the experience is as authentic as they come.

And then there's the Myvatn Nature Baths in the north. Smaller and less crowded than the Blue Lagoon, but just as beautiful, this place is a must-visit. The water is warm and soothing, the views are stunning, and the tranquility is just the thing to soothe a weary traveler's soul.

Cultural Experiences And Festivals

Now, if you were to ask me, "What's the first thing that pops into your head when you think of Iceland?" I'd say, "Well, I reckon it would be the music." The land of fire and ice is not just home to breathtaking landscapes, but also to a vibrant music scene. One cannot mention Iceland without a nod to the ethereal tunes of Björk or the post-rock melodies of Sigur Rós. The annual Iceland Airwaves music festival is a magnet for music lovers worldwide, boasting an eclectic mix of local and international acts. It's a grand spectacle, my friend, where the frosty Icelandic air resonates with foot-tapping beats and soul-stirring melodies.

Next on our cultural exploration, let's talk about literature. Icelanders are a bookish lot, I tell you. The nation has more writers, more books published and more books read per head than anywhere else in the world. Every year in November, Reykjavík, the world's northernmost capital, hosts the International Literary Festival. Authors, poets, and literature enthusiasts gather around, sharing stories, sipping on hot mead, and discussing the nuances of Icelandic sagas. It's a sight to behold, somewhat like watching a flock of birds in harmonious flight, each with a tale to tell.

If you're a film enthusiast, you're in luck. The Reykjavík International Film Festival is a haven for independent cinema. It's a smorgasbord of creativity, where filmmakers from all corners of the globe come together to showcase their craft.

Experiences and Adventures

Imagine sitting in a cozy theater, popcorn in hand, watching a captivating film roll while the northern lights dance in the sky outside. Sounds like a dream, doesn't it? Well, in Iceland, it's a reality.

And let's not forget the food. Iceland's culinary scene is a delightful blend of traditional and modern. The annual Food and Fun festival in Reykjavík is a gastronomic delight where renowned chefs from around the world compete to create innovative dishes using only Icelandic ingredients. It's like watching a painter create a masterpiece, but instead of paint, they use flavors, and instead of a canvas, they use a plate.

Iceland also has a unique tradition called Þorrablót. It's a mid-winter feast where locals gather to dine on traditional Icelandic fare like fermented shark, boiled sheep's head, and dried fish. It might not sound appetizing to the uninitiated, but it's a cultural experience that's worth a try. It's like a roller coaster ride - a little scary at first, but the thrill is something you wouldn't want to miss.

1. Þjóðhátíð (National Festival)
- **Location:** Westman Islands
- **Timing:** Annually during the first weekend in August
- **Description:** Þjóðhátíð is Iceland's largest outdoor festival, where Icelanders celebrate their national identity with music, fireworks, and camping. The festival is known for its incredible community spirit and spectacular firework displays.

2. Reykjavik Arts Festival
- **Location:** Reykjavik
- **Timing:** Biennially in May
- **Description:** This is a major event in Icelandic culture, showcasing both established and emerging Icelandic artists as well as international acts. It includes a wide range of art forms, from visual arts and design to music and theatre.

3. The Icelandic Saga Festivals
- **Location:** Various, including Reykholt and Thingvellir
- **Timing:** Summer months
- **Description:** These festivals celebrate Iceland's medieval history, particularly the Sagas. Events typically feature reenactments, lectures, and guided tours that delve into Viking history and mythology.

4. Secret Solstice Festival
- **Location:** Reykjavik
- **Timing:** Around the summer solstice in June
- **Description:** Coinciding with the 24 hours of daylight, this music festival offers a unique way to experience Icelandic music and international acts in an atmospheric setting under the midnight sun.

5. Reykjavik Pride
- **Location:** Reykjavik
- **Timing:** Annually in August
- **Description:** One of Iceland's most vibrant and popular events, Reykjavik Pride celebrates the LGBTQ+ community with a parade, concerts, and parties. It's known for its inclusivity and is a joyful expression of freedom and equality.

6. The Great Fish Day (Fiskidagurinn Mikli)
- **Location:** Dalvik
- **Timing:** Annually in August
- **Description:** A celebration of Iceland's fishing industry, this festival offers visitors the chance to taste freshly cooked fish for free, provided by the local fishermen, alongside a day of music and family-friendly entertainment.

7. Iceland Airwaves Music Festival
- **Location:** Reykjavik
- **Timing:** Annually in November
- **Description:** Iceland Airwaves is known for showcasing new music, both Icelandic and international. It's held across various venues in Reykjavik and is an essential stop for music lovers wanting to discover the next big thing.

8. DesignMarch
- **Location:** Reykjavik
- **Timing:** Annually in March
- **Description:** Iceland's premier design festival features four days of exhibitions, workshops, and lectures that highlight the best in local and international design, from fashion to furniture.

9. RIFF – Reykjavik International Film Festival
- **Location:** Reykjavik
- **Timing:** Annually in September-October
- **Description:** RIFF brings international and local filmmakers together, screening innovative films that often focus on up-and-coming directors. It offers a platform for networking and is a key event for film enthusiasts.

10. Winter Lights Festival
- **Location:** Reykjavik
- **Timing:** Annually in February
- **Description:** This festival is designed to spark the city with light and life during the darkest months of the year. Events include light installations, cultural events, and the popular Museum Night when museums across the city open their doors for free.

Family-Friendly Activities

Now, if you're toting along some of those young whippersnappers, don't you fret none. Iceland's got a whole heap of fun just waiting to be had by the young and the young at heart. Yes, sir, this land of fire and ice is just brimming with activities that'll have your little ones grinning from ear to ear.

First off, there's the whale watching. Now, I ain't talking about staring at your Uncle Eustace after he's had too much of Aunt Bertha's apple pie. I'm talking about real, live whales, the kind that make you gasp and point and forget you ever had a worry in the world. These majestic creatures of the deep blue sea are a sight to behold, and there's plenty of tours that'll get you up close and personal with them. Just make sure the young'uns don't try to pet 'em.

Next up, we have the puffin tours. Now, these ain't your regular birds. No, sir, these are birds with character, birds with charm. They're the jesters of the avian world, with their bright beaks and waddling walk. A puffin tour is like a comedy show, only the stars are feathered and the jokes are in squawks. It's a holler and a half, and the kids will love it.

If your brood is the adventurous sort, why not try some horse riding? Icelandic horses are a friendly bunch, sturdy and strong, just like the people here. They'll carry you and your family across lava fields, through green valleys and along black sand beaches. It's a fine way to see the countryside, and you might just make a four-legged friend while you're at it.

Now, if you're hankering for some culture, you can't go wrong with the Viking World museum. It's got a real Viking ship, the kind that the old Norsemen used to sail across the seas. There's also exhibits on Viking life and culture, so it's educational too. The kids will be so enthralled, they won't even realize they're learning.

1 Puffin Watching in Reykjavik:
- **Location:** Tours typically depart from Reykjavik's Old Harbour.
- **Price:** Around $40-$60 per adult, with discounts for children ages 7-15; free for younger children.
- **Details:** The tours last about 1 hour, making them suitable for younger children. Best time to visit is from May to August.

2 The Golden Circle Tour:
- **Location:** Starts and ends in Reykjavik, covering Þingvellir National Park, the Geysir Geothermal Area, and Gullfoss Waterfall.
- **Price:** Around $50-$100 per person; lower prices for children depending on the tour operator.
- **Details:** Full-day tour, generally about 6-8 hours, with frequent stops for short walks and photos.

3 Whale Watching in Husavik:

- **Location**: Husavik, North Iceland.
- **Price**: Approximately $80-$110 per adult, with child rates about half; under 7s often free.
- **Details**: Tours last 2-3 hours. Best visiting months are from April to October. Boats are equipped with safety gear and often have indoor viewing areas.

4 Visit to the Lava Centre:

- **Location**: Hvolsvöllur, Southern Iceland.
- **Price**: About $25 for adults, $12 for children aged 5-12, free for under 5s.
- **Details**: Interactive exhibits suitable for all ages, open year-round, takes about 1-2 hours to explore.

5 Family Horse Riding Near Reykjavik:

- **Location**: Various farms around Reykjavik and beyond.
- **Price**: Typically $50-$100 per person, depending on the duration and specific tour.
- **Details**: Tours can last from 1 to 4 hours, suitable for beginners and children over the age of 5.

6 The Wonders of Snæfellsnes Peninsula:

- **Location**: West Iceland, about a 2-hour drive from Reykjavik.
- **Price**: Self-driven tours are the cost of car rental and gas; guided tours range from $100-$150 per person.
- **Details**: Day-long trip, features attractions like Kirkjufell Mountain and Arnarstapi village, ideal for self-guided exploration with a rented vehicle.

7 Swimming in the Blue Lagoon or Local Geothermal Pools:

- **Location**: Blue Lagoon near Grindavík or local pools in various towns.
- **Price**: Blue Lagoon starts at about $50 per adult, with variable child prices; local pools are around $5-$15.
- **Details**: Blue Lagoon requires bookings in advance. Local pools are less crowded and have family-friendly facilities.

8 Exploring the Ice Caves and Glaciers:

- **Location**: Tours usually depart from near Skaftafell or Jökulsárlón in the southeast.
- **Price**: Around $100-$150 per person, depending on the tour type.
- **Details**: Suitable for children over 8 years old. Tours last about 2-3 hours, including preparation and safety briefings.

9 Visit to Hallgrimskirkja and Reykjavik City Tour:

- **Location**: Hallgrimskirkja located in central Reykjavik.
- **Price**: Free to enter the church; tower entry about $10 per adult, children free.
- **Details**: Church open year-round. The tower offers panoramic views of the city, and city tours can extend to several museums which offer family tickets.

10 Hiking in Landmannalaugar:

- **Location**: Highland region accessible by 4WD vehicles, about 3 hours from Reykjavik.
- **Price**: Free to hike; bus tours approximately $100 per person.
- **Details**: Best visited in summer (June to September). Day trips involve moderate hiking, so suitable for children who can handle a bit of a challenge.

Chapter 8
Local Cuisine

MUST-TRY DISHES

Now, I don't mean to startle you, but the first dish I'm going to recommend is something that you might not initially associate with fine dining, or indeed, dining at all. It's called hákarl, and it's fermented shark. Yes, you read that right. This national dish, steeped in tradition, is an acquired taste, much like a fine Scotch or a particularly pungent cheese. It's often served with a shot of Brennivín, a local schnapps, which, if you ask me, is a clever way to soften the blow of the shark's potent flavor.

Next on the list is harðfiskur, wind-dried fish, most commonly haddock, cod or catfish. It's eaten like jerky, often spread with butter. And I tell you, there's something about the mingling of the sea-salt breeze with the crunch of the dried fish that makes it a most delightful snack.

Now, if you're a fan of lamb, you're in for a treat. The Icelandic sheep roam freely, grazing on a smorgasbord of wild herbs and grasses, which lends the meat a flavor unparalleled elsewhere. Kjötsúpa, a traditional lamb soup, is a must-try. It's hearty, comforting, and will warm your bones after a day of exploring the geysers and glaciers.

Icelanders have a sweet tooth too, and the local dessert of choice is Skyr. This creamy, yoghurt-like substance has been a part of Icelandic cuisine for over a thousand years. It's often served with a sprinkling of sugar, a dash of cream, and a handful of berries. It's a dessert that's as simple as it is satisfying, and as sweet as the Icelandic summer days are long.

Local Cuisine

Icelandic rye bread, or rúgbrauð, is another gastronomic delight. It's dark, dense and slightly sweet, often baked in the ground using geothermal heat. Pair it with some Icelandic butter, and you'll have a culinary experience that's as close to the Icelandic soil as you can get without actually eating the dirt itself.

Lastly, let's talk drinks. Apart from the aforementioned Brennivín, Icelanders are mad about their coffee. They drink it black, strong and frequently. It's a cultural staple, much like discussing the weather or speculating on the where-abouts of elves.

And speaking of elves, there's a local beer, brewed with water from a glacier that's said to be home to these mythical creatures. It's called Kaldi, and it's a delightfully crisp lager that's as refreshing as a dip in one of Iceland's many hot springs.

1 Hákarl (Fermented Shark)

- **Description:** Made from the Greenland shark, this dish involves burying the shark underground for weeks to ferment and then hanging it to dry for several months. The result is a strong, ammonia-rich flavor.

- **Local Reception**: It remains a point of national pride for many Icelanders, especially older generations, though not all locals eat it regularly.
- **Tourist Reception**: Tourists often try hákarl out of curiosity; it's considered a challenging dish due to its pungent smell and taste.
- **Tradition and History**: Hákarl has been a part of Icelandic survival since the Viking Age, when food preservation options were limited. Its preparation method made the otherwise poisonous shark safe to eat.

2 Harðfiskur (Wind-Dried Fish)

- **Description**: Fish (typically haddock, cod, or catfish) that's been dried in the cold Icelandic air. It has a chewy texture and is often eaten as a snack, spread with butter.
- **Local Reception**: It's a popular snack among Icelanders, appreciated for its high protein content and convenience.
- **Tourist Reception**: Visitors often enjoy it as a unique, healthy snack. It's much more palatable to foreigners compared to hákarl.
- **Tradition and History**: Like hákarl, harðfiskur dates back to the Viking Age and was a vital method for preserving fish in Iceland's harsh climate.

3 Kjötsúpa (Traditional Lamb Soup)

- **Description**: A hearty soup made with lamb and a variety of root vegetables such as potatoes, carrots, and rutabaga, often seasoned with local herbs.
- **Local Reception**: Still widely consumed, especially during the colder months, as it is filling and warming.
- **Tourist Reception**: Tourists appreciate this dish for its comforting flavors and as an introduction to Icelandic home cooking.
- **Tradition and History**: This dish reflects Iceland's agricultural practices, showcasing the country's quality lamb, which is free-grazed across vast pastures.

4 Skyr (Icelandic Yogurt-Like Dessert)

- **Description**: A thick, creamy dairy product similar to yogurt but with a milder flavor. It is high in protein and often served with sugar, cream, and berries.
- **Local Reception**: Skyr is a staple in Icelandic diets, consumed at all times of the day.
- **Tourist Reception**: Visitors often enjoy skyr for its versatility and as a healthier alternative to traditional desserts.
- **Tradition and History**: Skyr has been consumed in Iceland for over a thousand years. It originated during the settlement of Iceland in the 9th century and was a vital source of nutrition.

5 Rúgbrauð (Icelandic Rye Bread)

- **Description**: A dark, dense, sweet rye bread traditionally baked in the ground near hot springs. The slow baking process results in a moist, cake-like texture.

- **Local Reception**: It remains a beloved component of the Icelandic diet, often eaten with fish, hangikjöt (smoked lamb), or butter.
- **Tourist Reception**: Tourists are fascinated by the unique method of geothermal baking and enjoy the bread's distinct flavor.
- **Tradition and History**: The practice of baking rúgbrauð in geothermal areas dates back centuries, utilizing Iceland's abundant geothermal energy as a natural oven.

6 Brennivín (Local Schnapps)

- **Description**: A clear, unsweetened schnapps made from fermented potato mash and flavored with caraway seeds. It's considered Iceland's signature distilled beverage.
- **Local Reception**: Often consumed during festive occasions, particularly the mid-winter feast known as Þorrablót.
- **Tourist Reception**: Known as "Black Death," it's a must-try for visitors looking to experience traditional Icelandic spirits.
- **Tradition and History**: Brennivín has been around since the 18th century and was originally introduced as a remedy for various ailments.

7 Plokkfiskur (Fish Stew)

- **Description**: This comforting stew is made from boiled fish (often cod or haddock), potatoes, onions, and bechamel sauce. It's typically served with rye bread and butter.
- **Local Reception**: Plokkfiskur is a beloved comfort food in Iceland, often enjoyed at home and found in traditional restaurants.
- **Tourist Reception**: Tourists appreciate this dish for its creamy, hearty flavor, which makes it a satisfying meal, especially in cold weather.
- **Tradition and History**: Historically, plokkfiskur was a practical way to use leftover fish and make it stretch further. It reflects the Icelandic emphasis on not wasting food and utilizing local ingredients efficiently.

8 Hangikjöt (Smoked Lamb)

- **Description**: Lamb meat that is smoked with traditional Icelandic methods, often involving dried sheep dung to give it a distinct flavor. It's served sliced, either hot or cold, and often accompanied by peas, red cabbage, and béchamel sauce.
- **Local Reception**: Hangikjöt is a staple during the Christmas season and other celebrations, revered for its rich, smoky flavor.
- **Tourist Reception**: Visitors are usually eager to try this unique smoked meat, appreciating its cultural significance and distinctive taste.
- **Tradition and History**: Smoking with sheep dung is a technique born out of necessity in a tree-scarce land and has been practiced for centuries to preserve meat through the harsh winters.

9 Kleinur (Icelandic Doughnut)

- **Description**: A twisted doughnut made of a slightly sweetened dough that is fried until golden. Kleinur has a crunchy exterior and a soft, airy interior, often flavored with cardamom.
- **Local Reception**: Kleinur is a popular snack or dessert, commonly enjoyed with coffee during the afternoon.
- **Tourist Reception**: Tourists love trying kleinur as it offers a taste of Icelandic home baking that's different from typical American-style doughnuts.
- **Tradition and History**: This treat has roots in Scandinavian baking and has been a part of Icelandic cuisine for generations, illustrating the cultural exchange through food.

10 Svið (Sheep's Head)

- **Description**: A traditional dish where a sheep's head is cut in half, singed to remove the fur, and then boiled with the brain removed. It's typically served with mashed potatoes and mashed turnip.
- **Local Reception**: While not as commonly eaten on a daily basis anymore, svið is still respected as a traditional dish, particularly among older generations and during Þorrablót, the Icelandic midwinter festival.
- **Tourist Reception**: Definitely an acquired taste, svið challenges many tourists due to its appearance and concept, but trying it can be seen as a rite of passage.
- **Tradition and History**: Svið dates back to times when no part of the animal was wasted. It's a testament to the resourcefulness of traditional Icelandic culinary practices.

Dining Etiquette

Now, Icelanders take their meal times quite seriously, but not in the stuffy, starched-collar way that those English do. No, sir. Instead, they've got a sort of relaxed formality about them. A gentleman or lady might stroll into a restaurant clad in hiking boots and a parka, and no one would bat an eye. But try to start your meal before everyone's got their food, and you'll have the whole room staring at you like you've just walked in wearing a Viking helmet.

Speaking of helmets, let's talk about hats. In Iceland, it's considered polite to remove your hat at the table, unless you're dining outdoors. If you're dining in the wild under the Northern Lights, then by all means, keep your hat on. You wouldn't want to catch a cold while you're trying to enjoy your pickled herring.

Now, about that herring. Icelandic cuisine can be a bit, well, adventurous for some palates. You've got your fermented shark, your sheep's head, and your dried fish. But don't go turning up your nose just yet. Remember, this is a country where they eat hot dogs as a national pastime. And believe me, if you can stomach a hot dog from a New York street vendor, you can handle a little fermented shark.

When it comes to the bill, Icelanders believe in splitting it evenly. So, if you've decided to go for the lobster while your companion has stuck with the soup, you might want to offer to cover a bit more of the bill. If not, you might find yourself on the receiving end of some icy Nordic glares.

And one last thing, my friends. If you find yourself invited to an Icelander's home for a meal, don't forget to say "Gjörðu svo vel" before you start eating. It's their way of saying "Bon appétit," and it's sure to earn you a few appreciative nods from your hosts.

- **Dress Code**: Informal attire is acceptable in most dining settings. Feel free to wear hiking boots and a parka to a restaurant.
- **Meal Commencement**: Wait until everyone at your table has received their food before starting to eat.
- **Hats Off**: It is customary to remove your hat at the table when indoors. Keep your hat on if dining outside, especially in cold conditions.
- **Adventurous Cuisine**: Be open to trying traditional dishes like fermented shark, sheep's head, and dried fish. Remember, these are all part of the local culinary experience.
- **Bill Splitting**: The bill is usually split evenly among all diners, regardless of individual orders. Consider offering to pay more if your meal was significantly pricier than others'.
- **Local Courtesy**: If invited to a local's home, say "Gjörðu svo vel" before eating to express your gratitude and readiness to dine, akin to "Bon appétit."
- **Remember**: Embrace the local food and customs; every meal is an opportunity to learn and create stories.

Best Dining Experiences In Iceland

First off, let's talk about the infamous hákarl, or fermented shark. Now, don't turn up your nose just yet! This dish is a proud badge of honor for any self-respecting foodie who dares to venture in the land of ice and fire. The shark is buried underground to ferment for several months before it is hung to dry. The resulting dish, my dear reader, is an olfactory assault that is as much a rite of passage as it is a meal. But fear not, a swig of the local spirit, Brennivín, also fondly known as 'Black Death', will help you wash down the shark and your apprehensions along with it!

Speaking of spirits, the Icelandic beer scene is a wonder in its own right. With the prohibition on beer only lifted in 1989, the Icelanders have wasted no time in brewing up a storm. Microbreweries are sprouting up faster than mushrooms after a rain shower, each offering their unique take on the golden brew. Whether you fancy a classic lager or a fruity IPA, the Icelandic beer scene has got you covered.

If you are more of a landlubber when it comes to your food, then the Icelandic lamb should be right up your alley. Raised free-range and fed on a diet of berries, herbs, and moss, these lambs produce a meat that is tender, flavorful, and as close to organic as you can get. Cooked over an open fire, this is a dish that harkens back to the Viking age, and one that you absolutely must try.

Now, for those with a sweet tooth, let me introduce you to Skyr. This yogurt-like dairy product has been a staple in the Icelandic diet for over a thousand years. Low in fat yet high in protein, it is a healthy treat that can be enjoyed with a dollop of honey or a sprinkle of granola.

And let's not forget about the seafood. The cold Atlantic waters that surround Iceland are teeming with a variety of fish and shellfish. From the traditional Plokkfiskur, a comforting fish stew, to the more modern sushi, the Icelandic seafood is as fresh as it gets.

To round off your culinary journey, make sure to visit one of the many coffee houses in Reykjavik. The Icelanders take their coffee very seriously, and this is evident in the quality of the brew. A cup of Icelandic coffee is the perfect way to warm up after a day of exploring the glaciers.

Feature on Festive Dishes:
- **Laufabrauð (Delicate Fried Bread):** Often referred to as "leaf bread," laufabrauð is intricately decorated with geometric patterns and fried to a delicate crispness. It is a festive favorite, particularly during Christmas, symbolizing the joy and artistry of the season. The tradition of cutting laufabrauð is a family affair, with each pattern as unique as the hands that crafted them.
- **Hangikjöt (Smoked Lamb):** A savory highlight at any Icelandic Christmas table, hangikjöt is lamb that has been smoked over birch or dried sheep dung, imparting a unique flavor deeply embedded in Icelandic culinary traditions. This dish is typically served cold and sliced thin, accompanied by rye bread, béchamel sauce, or green peas.
- **Bollur (Sweet Icelandic Doughnuts):** These are not your average dough-nuts. Bollur are richly filled with jam or cream and heartily dusted with sugar, a special treat savored during the festive season, especially on Bolludagur, or Bun Day, signaling the beginning of Lent.

Where and When to Experience These Foods:
- **Þorrablót Celebrations:** Held in late January or early February, this is the perfect time to dive into the heart of Icelandic culinary tradition. Many restau-rants and local communities host special Þorrablót evenings where dishes like hákarl (fermented shark) and svið (sheep's head) accompany the aforementioned festive foods.

- **Christmas Markets:** Visit the Christmas markets in Reykjavik, such as the one at Ingólfstorg Square, to taste laufabrauð and bollur. The markets usually begin in late November and provide a festive atmosphere filled with the scent of smoked lamb and sweet treats.
- **Specialty Restaurants:** For an authentic taste of hangikjöt throughout the year, seek out traditional Icelandic restaurants that specialize in local cuisine. Restaurants in Reykjavik like "Íslenski Barinn" offer a contemporary twist on these classics, providing a culinary bridge from past to present.

Iceland's extensive coastline is a treasure trove of culinary delights, profoundly influencing local diets with its bounty of fresh seafood. The cold, clear waters of the North Atlantic are home to a diverse range of marine life, ensuring that seafood is not only a staple but a highlight of the Icelandic table.

Exploring Local Seafood Markets:

A visit to Fiskmarkaðurinn, Reykjavik's main fish market, is essential for seafood enthusiasts. Here, you can observe the vibrant hustle of daily auctions, engage with local fishermen, and learn about the variety of seafood harvested from Icelandic waters, such as cod, haddock, and the coveted Icelandic langoustine.

Recommended Seafood Restaurants:

- **Fiskfélagið (Fish Company) in Reykjavik:** Known for its innovative dishes like Arctic char with mango and chili salsa.
- **Pakkhús in Höfn:** Specializes in Icelandic lobster, offering it in a range of dishes from simple grilled preparations to rich, creamy pastas.
- **Tjöruhúsið in Ísafjörður:** Famous for its fish stew and fresh catches of the day, served in a cozy, communal setting.
- **Fjöruborðið in Stokkseyri:** Offers a memorable dining experience with its blue mussels steamed to perfection, enjoyed with views of the sea.

Vegan And Vegetarian Options

Iceland, it seems, has been paying heed to the whispers of the world. The small but mighty island is increasingly accommodating those of the leaf-loving persuasion. In the capital city of Reykjavik, one can find a plethora of establishments offering meatless meals.

Among these, Glo stands out like a beacon in the night. It's a veritable Eden for the herbivores amongst us, offering a smorgasbord of salads, soups, wraps, and even raw food options. They've got enough greens to make a rabbit swoon, and their dishes are as pleasing to the eye as they are to the palate.

For those who prefer a bit of international flair, there's Kaffi Vinyl, a hip and happening spot that serves up vegan versions of dishes from around the globe.

Fancy a taste of Italy? Their lasagna is a symphony of flavors that would make a nonna proud. Got a hankering for something a bit more exotic? Their Vietnamese pho is a bowlful of comfort that'll warm your cockles, even in the depths of an Icelandic winter.

But what about those times when the craving for traditional Icelandic fare strikes? Fret not, for there are places that cater to this particular palate too. At Kaffihus Vesturbæjar, one can indulge in vegan versions of Icelandic classics. Their vegan 'fish' and chips is a dish that confounds the senses in the best possible way, while their vegetable stew is a hearty concoction that would make even the most stubborn meat-eater reconsider their life choices.

The supermarkets too, have not been left behind in this green revolution. Many carry a variety of vegan and vegetarian products, from dairy-free milks and cheeses, to meat substitutes and even vegan caviar! Yes, you read that right. In Iceland, even the fish eggs are plant-based.

One mustn't forget the bakeries either. Many a morning can be made brighter with a visit to Braud & Co. Their vegan pastries are a delight to the senses and a testament to the fact that butter and eggs do not a good pastry make. Their cinnamon rolls, in particular, are a thing of beauty - soft, sticky, and sinfully delicious.

Reykjavik
1 Dill Restaurant
- **Location**: Hverfisgata 12
- **Highlights**: The first Icelandic restaurant to receive a Michelin star, Dill offers a menu that changes weekly, focusing on innovative Nordic cuisine.

2 Grillmarkaðurinn (Grill Market)
- **Location**: Lækjargata 2A
- **Highlights**: Known for its use of local ingredients such as Icelandic lamb, seafood, and wild game, this restaurant provides a unique twist on traditional grilling.

3 Matur og Drykkur
- **Location**: Grandagarður 2
- **Highlights**: Specializes in classic Icelandic recipes with a modern touch, ideal for those looking to explore traditional dishes like cod head cooked in chicken broth.

Akureyri
4 Bautinn
- **Location**: Hafnarstræti 92
- **Highlights**: A cozy place to enjoy hearty Icelandic comfort food at reasonable prices, with a menu that features the best of local fish and meats.

5 Rub23

Local Cuisine

- **Location**: Kaupvangsstræti 6
- **Highlights**: Known for its unique sushi and seafood dishes, Rub23 uses ingredients from Icelandic waters with a mix of Japanese and Icelandic cooking techniques.

Höfn
6 Pakkhús Restaurant

- **Location**: Hafnarbraut 4
- **Highlights**: Overlooking the harbor, this restaurant specializes in locally sourced seafood, particularly langoustines, offering a true taste of Höfn.

Keflavík
7 Kaffi Duus

- **Location**: Duusgata 10
- **Highlights**: Offers spectacular views of the marina and serves a wide array of dishes, with a focus on fresh fish and shellfish caught daily from the nearby waters.

Húsavík
8 Naustið

- **Location**: Garðarsbraut 6
- **Highlights**: This small, charming restaurant is renowned for its fresh seafood soup and homemade bread, providing a warm, rustic dining experience.

Ísafjörður
9 Tjöruhúsið

- **Location**: Neðstikaupstað
- **Highlights**: Set in an old tar house, this place is famous for its fish stew and fresh fish dishes, served buffet-style in a convivial atmosphere.

Vik
10 Sudur Vik

- **Location**: Klettsvegi 1-5
- **Highlights**: Boasts a great view of Reynisfjara and the Reynisdrangar pillars, serving excellent pizzas and local dishes in a cozy setting.

And to the carnivores reading this, I urge you to step outside your comfort zone. Give the green side a chance. You never know, you might just find that the grass is indeed, greener on the other side. After all, in a country where the impossible becomes possible, who's to say you can't enjoy a meatless meal?

Chapter 9
Exploration Guides

DAY TRIPS FROM REYKJAVÍK

Now, if you're anything like me, you might be thinking, "But I'm in Reykjavík! Isn't that enough?" Well, dear reader, I'm here to tell you that while Reykjavík is indeed a marvel, the rest of Iceland is not to be overlooked. It's like having a delicious loaf of bread but ignoring the butter and jam. Sure, you could do it, but why on earth would you want to?

Firstly, there's the Golden Circle, a tourist route that covers about 300 kilometers and loops from Reykjavík into central Iceland and back. It's called the Golden Circle, not because it's made of gold (which would indeed be quite a sight), but because it encompasses several of Iceland's most stunning natural wonders. These include the Thingvellir National Park, the Gullfoss waterfall, and the geothermal area in Haukadalur, which houses the geyser Geysir. If you're not one for long travels, fear not! This trip can easily be accomplished in a day.

Next, there's the **South Coast**, home to some of the most breathtaking landscapes you'll ever lay your eyes on. Black sand beaches, majestic waterfalls, glaciers – it's as though Mother Nature herself decided to show off. If you're feeling particularly adventurous, you might even take a walk behind the Seljalandsfoss waterfall. Just make sure you've got a waterproof coat, or you'll end up wetter than a fish in the Atlantic.

If you're a fan of wildlife, then the Snaefellsnes Peninsula is the place for you. Here, you can spot seals lounging on the beaches, birds nesting on the cliffs, and if you're very lucky, you might even see a whale or two in the distance. The Peninsula is also home to the Snaefellsjokull glacier, a sight so beautiful it could bring a tear to a glass eye.

And then, there's the Blue Lagoon, a geothermal spa located in a lava field. The waters are rich in minerals and supposedly have healing properties. Whether that's true or not, I can't say, but what I can say is that there's nothing quite like soaking in warm water while surrounded by the stark beauty of a lava field.

The Golden Circle Route

Why, if you find yourself in Iceland, you must surely take the time to traverse the Golden Circle Route. It's a roguish loop of road, barely a hundred kilometers from the capital, Reykjavik. Now, I'm not one to demand, but this is a trip that's not to be missed, I tell you!

You'll start your journey at Thingvellir National Park, a place so full of history it practically hums with it. You see, this was where the world's first parliament was established, way back in 930 AD. And if that isn't enough to tickle your fancy, the park is also a geological wonder, straddling two tectonic plates. You can actually walk between North America and Europe. Now, how many can boast that they've had one foot in two continents at the same time?

Next, you'll traipse over to the Geysir geothermal area. Now, this is a place that'll truly blow your top off, quite literally! The Great Geysir, though a bit of a sleeping giant these days, was once known to shoot water up to 70 meters in the air. Its more active neighbor, Strokkur, reliably erupts every few minutes, providing a spectacle that's sure to make your eyes pop and your camera shutter work overtime.

Your last stop, but by no means the least, is the Gullfoss waterfall. Now, when I say waterfall, don't imagine a little trickle of water over some rocks. No, sir! Gullfoss is a thunderous, two-tiered waterfall that'll make your heart race and your spirit soar. There's a raw, unbridled power to it that'll leave you feeling small and wonderfully insignificant.

Now, along this route, you won't be left starving, I promise. There are plenty of places to fill your belly and wet your whistle. One such place is Fridheimar, a charming tomato farm where you can enjoy a warm, tomato-based lunch under the glow of the greenhouses. The bread, lathered with cucumber salsa, is a delight, and the tomato soup, why it's as comforting as a mother's hug on a cold day. And if you're feeling a little adventurous, try the tomato beer. It's an odd combination, I'll grant, but one that works surprisingly well.

And if you've got a sweet tooth, Efstidalur II is the place for you. This family-run farm offers homemade ice cream that'll have you moaning with pleasure. The flavors change with the seasons, but the quality, oh the quality never wavers. It's the sort of ice cream that'll ruin you for all other ice creams.

Exploring The Ring Road

Now, before you go packing your bags and lacing your boots, do bear in mind that this is no Sunday afternoon drive. No siree! This is a journey of over 800 miles, and it will take you a good week, if not more, to traverse its length. But fear not, for the rewards are as plentiful as the miles are long.

You'll find yourself in awe as you navigate the serpentine twists and turns of the road, with nothing but the open sky and the raw, untouched beauty of nature as your companions. It's as if Mother Nature herself took a paintbrush and splashed her finest work across this canvas of land and sky.

The first stop on this grand tour is the capital city of Reykjavik, where you can whet your appetite with an assortment of local delicacies. From hákarl (fermented shark) to pylsur (Icelandic hot dogs), the city offers a gastronomical adventure that's sure to tickle your taste buds.

From there, the road will lead you to the Snæfellsnes Peninsula, a place so enchanting it's been dubbed 'Iceland in Miniature'. Here, you can marvel at the Snæfellsjökull Glacier, a frozen giant that's inspired many a tale and legend.

Further along, you'll encounter the mighty Dettifoss, a waterfall so powerful, it's been crowned the 'Beast' to its southern counterpart, Goðafoss, the 'Beauty'. Now, if that doesn't stir your adventurous spirit, I don't know what will!

You'll also pass through the otherworldly landscapes of the Mývatn region, where you can take a dip in the geothermal baths and let the warm, mineral-rich waters soothe your weary bones.

And let's not forget the charming coastal towns dotted along the way, each with its own unique charm and character. From the picturesque fishing village of Höfn to the quaint town of Egilsstaðir, these stops offer a welcome respite from the road and a chance to sample the local fare.

But, dear reader, the Ring Road is more than just a highway; it's a journey into the heart of Iceland, a glimpse into its soul. It's a testament to the resilience of the land and its people, who have carved out a life amidst the elements.

Off-The-Beaten-Path Adventures

When you've had your fill of the typical tourist trails and the beaten paths of Iceland, your soul might start yearning for something a tad more adventurous and less discovered, something that might make your heart race just a bit faster. Well, fear not, for Iceland is full of such hidden treasures, waiting to be discovered by the more adventurous among us.

Now, imagine this: you're standing at the entrance of a cave, its mouth gaping wide and dark, almost daring you to step in. This isn't just any cave, mind you. This is Lofthellir, a lava cave located in the north-east part of the country. As you step in, you might find yourself in a world of ice and darkness, the light from your torch illuminating strange and wonderful ice formations. These formations have been formed over centuries, a silent testament to the passage of time. It's a sight to behold, I assure you.

Or perhaps, you'd fancy a visit to the abandoned village of Selatangar. Located on the Reykjanes Peninsula, this settlement was abandoned in the 19th century. Today, it stands as a ghost town, its stone walls and structures standing as a silent reminder of the harsh living conditions of the past. Walking through the village, one can almost hear whispers of the past, tales of hardy fishermen and their daily struggles. It's not a place for the faint-hearted, but for those who dare, it's a journey back in time.

Then, there's the hidden hot spring of Reykjadalur. Located in a valley not far from the town of Hveragerdi, this hot spring is a well-kept secret. The hike to get there might be a bit demanding, but the reward is well worth it. Imagine soaking in a natural hot spring, surrounded by the untouched beauty of the Icelandic landscape. It's a moment of pure bliss, a chance to connect with nature in its rawest form.

And who can forget the Westfjords? This remote region is often overlooked by travelers, but those who venture there are rewarded with an untouched paradise. From the stunning cliffs of Látrabjarg, home to millions of seabirds, to the pristine beaches of Rauðasandur, the Westfjords are a haven for those seeking solitude and tranquility.

Finally, for those with a taste for the mysterious, there's the Hólmanes nature reserve. Legends say that this place is inhabited by elves and other supernatural beings. Whether you believe in these tales or not, there's no denying the magic of Hólmanes. With its diverse birdlife and unique rock formations, it's a place that captivates the mind and soothes the soul.

Day 1: Arrival in Reykjavik

- **Arrival:** Land at Keflavík International Airport (KEF) at 08:00 AM.
- **Transportation:** Rent a car from the airport. Multiple rental services are available right at the airport, offering a range of vehicles suited to Icelandic roads.
- **Accommodation:** Check into Icelandair Hotel Reykjavik Marina, Mýrargata 2, 101 Reykjavík (Tel: +354 560 8000). Check-in time is 3:00 PM.
- **Activities:**
- 11:00 AM: Visit the Blue Lagoon, 240 Grindavík (Advance booking required, Tel: +354 420 8800). Enjoy relaxing in the geothermal waters.
- 7:00 PM: Dinner at Grillmarkaðurinn, Lækjargata 2A, 101 Reykjavík (Tel: +354 571 7777).
- **Emergency Contacts:**
- General Emergency: 112
- U.S. Embassy: Laufásvegur 21, 101 Reykjavík (Tel: +354 595 2200)

Day 2: Golden Circle Tour

- **Departure:** Leave hotel at 09:00 AM.
- **Transportation:** Drive yourself; the Golden Circle is a well-marked route suitable for self-driving.
- **Activities:**
- 10:00 AM: Þingvellir National Park, Þingvellir (Park for 2 hours).
- 1:00 PM: Lunch at Geysir Glima Restaurant, Geysir (Tel: +354 480 6800).
- 2:30 PM: Visit Geysir Hot Springs and Gullfoss Waterfall.
- **Return to Reykjavik:** Expected arrival at hotel by 8:00 PM.

Day 3: South Coast Adventure

- **Departure:** Leave hotel at 08:00 AM.
- **Transportation:** Self-drive.

- **Activities**:
- 10:30 AM: Seljalandsfoss Waterfall.
- 12:30 PM: Lunch at Black Beach Restaurant, Vík í Mýrdal (Tel: +354 487 4900).
- 2:00 PM: Reynisfjara Black Sand Beach and the town of Vík.
- 5:00 PM: Skógafoss Waterfall.
- **Return to Reykjavik**: Expected arrival at hotel by 9:00 PM.

Day 4: Explore Reykjavik
- **Activities**:
- 10:00 AM: Visit Hallgrímskirkja, Hallgrímstorg 1, 101 Reykjavík.
- 12:00 PM: Lunch at Café Loki, Lokastígur 28, 101 Reykjavík (Tel: +354 466 2828).
- 2:00 PM: Explore the National Museum of Iceland, Suðurgata 41, 101 Reykjavík (Tel: +354 530 2200).
- 7:00 PM: Dinner at Matur og Drykkur, Grandagarður 2, 101 Reykjavík (Tel: +354 571 8877).

Day 5: Akureyri and Northern Iceland
- **Departure**: Catch an early flight to Akureyri from Reykjavík Domestic Airport at 07:00 AM.
- **Accommodation**: Check into Hotel Kea by Keahotels, Hafnarstræti 87-89, Akureyri (Tel: +354 460 2000). Check-in time is 3:00 PM.
- **Activities**:
- 9:00 AM: Visit Akureyri Botanical Garden, Eyrarlandsvegur, Akureyri.
- 12:00 PM: Lunch at Rub23, Kaupvangsstræti 6, Akureyri (Tel: +354 462 2223).
- 2:00 PM: Explore the town center and visit the Akureyri Church.
- 6:00 PM: Return flight to Reykjavik.
- **Return to Reykjavik**: Expected arrival at hotel by 8:00 PM.

Day 6: West Iceland and Snæfellsnes Peninsula
- **Departure**: Leave hotel at 08:00 AM.
- **Transportation**: Self-drive.
- **Activities**:
- 10:00 AM: Visit Kirkjufell Mountain and Waterfall.
- 1:00 PM: Lunch at Bjargarsteinn Mathús, Grundarfjörður (Tel: +354 438 6800).
- 3:00 PM: Explore Snæfellsjökull National Park.
- **Return to Reykjavik**: Expected arrival at hotel by 9:00 PM.

Day 7: Departure
- **Check-out**: Hotel check-out by 11:00 AM.

- **Transportation**: Drive back to Keflavík International Airport. Return rental car.
- **Departure**: Catch your return flight scheduled at 2:00 PM.

Day 8: Explore the Eastfjords
- **Departure**: Depart from Reykjavik early morning.
- **Transportation**: Drive to Eastfjords, approximately a 6-7 hour drive.
- **Accommodation**: Check into Fosshotel Eastfjords, Fáskrúðsfjörður (Tel +354 562 4000). Check-in time is 3:00 PM.
- **Activities**:
- 2:00 PM: Visit Petra's Stone Collection in Stöðvarfjörður.
- 4:00 PM: Explore the picturesque village of Seyðisfjörður.
- 7:00 PM: Dinner at Hotel Aldan in Seyðisfjörður (Tel: +354 472 1277).
- **Emergency Contacts**:
- Local Police: 112 (General Emergency Number)

Day 9: Hike and Relax in Eastfjords
- **Activities**:
- 10:00 AM: Hiking in the trails around Fáskrúðsfjörður.
- 1:00 PM: Lunch at a local café in Fáskrúðsfjörður.
- 3:00 PM: Relax in the hot springs found in the area, or explore more of the scenic landscapes.
- 7:00 PM: Dinner at Randulff's Sea-House, Eskifjörður (Tel: +354 476 1277).

Day 10: Travel to the Northern Capital, Akureyri
- **Departure**: Depart from Fosshotel Eastfjords at 08:00 AM.
- **Transportation**: Drive to Akureyri, approximately a 5-hour journey.
- **Accommodation**: Check back into Hotel Kea by Keahotels, Akureyri (Refer to Day 5 for details).
- **Activities**:
- 4:00 PM: Visit the Arctic Botanical Gardens (Lystigardurinn) in Akureyri if not done previously.
- 7:00 PM: Dinner at Strikið, Akureyri (Tel: +354 462 7100).

Day 11: Lake Mývatn Adventure
- **Departure**: Leave Akureyri at 09:00 AM.
- **Transportation**: Self-drive.
- **Activities**:
- 10:30 AM: Explore Lake Mývatn area, including Dimmuborgir and the Mývatn Nature Baths.
- 1:00 PM: Lunch at Vogafjós Farm Restaurant, Mývatn (Tel: +354 464 4303).
- 3:00 PM: Visit the Hverfjall crater for a light hike.
- 7:00 PM: Return to Akureyri.

Day 12: Whale Watching in Húsavík

- **Departure**: Depart from Akureyri at 08:00 AM.
- **Transportation**: Drive to Húsavík, approximately 1-hour drive.
- **Activities**:
- 10:00 AM: Go whale watching with a local tour operator, such as North Sailing (Tel: +354 464 7272).
- 1:00 PM: Lunch at Salka Restaurant in Húsavík (Tel: +354 464 2442).
- 3:00 PM: Visit the Húsavík Whale Museum.
- 6:00 PM: Return to Akureyri.

Day 13: Back to Reykjavik
- **Departure**: Leave Akureyri at 09:00 AM.
- **Transportation**: Fly back to Reykjavik from Akureyri Airport. Flight typically lasts 45 minutes.
- **Accommodation**: Check back into Icelandair Hotel Reykjavik Marina.
- **Activities**:
- Free afternoon to explore any missed attractions in Reykjavik or shop for souvenirs.
- 7:00 PM: Farewell dinner at Apotek Restaurant, Austurstræti 16, Reykjavík (Tel: +354 512 9000).

Day 14: Departure from Iceland
- **Check-out**: Hotel check-out by 11:00 AM.
- **Transportation**: Drive to Keflavík International Airport, about a 45-minute drive.
- **Departure**: Check in for your flight, ideally 2-3 hours before departure.

Chapter 10
Practical Information

EMERGENCY CONTACTS

In the unlikely event of a calamity, you might find yourself needing to call upon the good folks of Iceland's emergency services. Now, these ain't your everyday, run-of-the-mill emergency services. No siree! This is Iceland we're talking about. Their emergency services are as cool as the icebergs floating in Jökulsárlón lagoon and as hot as the magma bubbling beneath Eyjafjallajökull.

The number to dial in case of an emergency is 112. It's as easy as pie, isn't it? Just three digits, one, one, two. It's a number that's as simple as a child's lullaby, but as vital as the air you breathe.

Now, if you're in need of medical assistance, there's a separate number for that. Dial 1700 if you're calling from an Icelandic number. If you're calling from an international number, dial +354 544 4113. It's a trifle more complex than 112, but it's as necessary as a warm coat in an Icelandic winter.

For those of you who have a knack for getting lost, don't fret. The Icelandic Association for Search and Rescue (ICE-SAR) is ready and waiting to lend a helping hand. Just remember, these fine folks are volunteers who brave the elements to keep you safe. So, if you do find yourself in a pickle, use their services wisely and responsibly.

If you're ever in a situation where you need to report a crime, the number to call is 444 1000. Although, let's be honest here, the likelihood of that happening in Iceland is about as probable as finding a palm tree in the middle of Reykjavik.

For those of you who have a tendency to overindulge in Iceland's delightful culinary offerings and find yourself with a touch of food poisoning, the Directorate of Health has a poison hotline. The number to call is 800 1260. It's a number you'd wish you never have to use, but it's good to have just in case you mistake fermented shark for a slice of apple pie.

Currency, Payments, And Tipping

Now, onto the matter of payments. Icelanders are quite the modern folk, you see. Cash is as outdated as dial-up internet in this land of fire and ice. Plastic is the king here, and by that, I mean credit and debit cards. You can use them almost everywhere, from the quaintest coffee houses to the most remote gas stations. It's a convenience that would make even the most technologically-challenged traveler breathe a sigh of relief. But be not too quick to rejoice, for there's a catch. Make sure your card is equipped with a chip and a four-digit PIN, as the old swipe and sign method has been tossed into the history books alongside the Vikings.

Now, let's venture into the realm of tipping. If you are an American, you might be used to tipping everyone from your waiter to your hairdresser, but in Iceland, it's a whole different ball game. In fact, tipping is as rare as a sunny day in this land. You see, the Icelanders believe in paying their workers a fair wage, so there's no need for that extra bit of generosity. But of course, if the service you received was so splendid that it moved you to tears, then by all means, leave a tip! Just remember, it's not expected, and certainly not required.

Language Basics

Now, let's turn our attention to the linguistic side of things, the very tool that'll serve as your compass in this Nordic wonderland. Icelandic, my dear friends, is the language of the land, a tongue spun from the old Norse of yesteryears. It's a language that has seen the rise and fall of the sun for centuries, a language that has absorbed the whispers of the wind, the roars of the sea, and the quiet of the snow.

I know what you're thinking, "That sounds a bit too poetic and a smidge intimidating." Well, my dear reader, fear not! For as old and complex as it may seem, Icelandic is but a language, and like any language, it can be learned, understood, and even loved.

Now, before you start sweating at the thought of declensions, conjugations, and the like, let me tell you a little secret. Most Icelanders speak English. They do! Quite fluently too. So, if you're feeling a bit tongue-tied or if the words start looking like a jumbled mess of consonants, just switch to English. The locals won't mind, and they'll probably appreciate your effort in trying to speak their language.

However, that's not to say that you shouldn't give Icelandic a fair shot. Oh no, my dear reader, for there is a certain charm to speaking the language of the land. Imagine strolling down the streets of Reykjavik, greeting the locals with a hearty "Góðan daginn" (Good day) or thanking the shopkeeper with a sincere "Takk fyrir" (Thank you). It's these little moments, these tiny connections that truly enrich your travel experience.

Learning a few basic phrases won't hurt either. It's a sign of respect towards the local culture and a way to show your enthusiasm as a visitor. Not to mention, it can be quite handy in certain situations. For instance, knowing how to ask for directions, "Hvar er...?" (Where is...?) or being able to express your dietary preferences, "Ég er grænkeri" (I am a vegetarian), can make your Icelandic adventure smoother and more enjoyable.

Now, you might be wondering, "Where do I even start learning Icelandic?" Well, there are plenty of resources available online, from language learning apps to online courses. You could also pick up a phrasebook or two, which can be quite useful for quick references.

But remember, my dear reader, the goal here isn't to master Icelandic, unless of course, you're planning to settle down and become a local. Your aim should be to familiarize yourself with the sounds, the rhythm, and the feel of the language. It's about immersing yourself in the culture, about creating a connection, however small, with the land and its people.

Mobile And Internet Connectivity

Now, let's meander towards the topic of technological connectivity in this frosty wonderland. For you tech-savvy explorers out there, fear not! Iceland, despite its remote location and sometimes unforgiving climate, is as connected as a spider's web. Some might even say it's more akin to a bustling ant hill, with signals speeding back and forth like busy workers.

Firstly, let's jabber about mobile connectivity. Most of Iceland, including its vast and seemingly endless landscapes, enjoys good mobile coverage. The city slickers among you will be relieved to know that the capital, Reykjavik, boasts top-notch 4G coverage. You can snap, tweet, and post to your heart's content. However, for those venturing into the more remote parts of the island - yes, I'm looking at you, intrepid adventurers - coverage can be a tad patchy. But worry not, for the sight of the untouched wilderness will more than make up for a few missed notifications.

As for those of you concerned about roaming charges, Iceland, being a part of he European Economic Area, follows the 'Roam like at Home' rule. This means that EU citizens can use their mobile data at no extra cost. Non-EU travelers, however, I advise you to check with your service provider before you start streaming the Northern Lights live on Instagram!

Now, let's surf the waves of the Internet, shall we? Icelanders are a tech-savvy bunch, with one of the highest rates of Internet usage in the world. Wi-Fi is as common as geysers in Iceland. Most hotels, cafes, and even buses offer free Wi-Fi. So, you can easily upload your travelogue or check the weather forecast for your next expedition.

The speed of the Internet in Iceland is as swift as the Icelandic horses. The country ranks among the top in the world for Internet speed, thus making it an ideal destination for digital nomads. So, if you've been dreaming about working remotely while soaking in a geothermal pool, Iceland might just be the place for you!

But do remember, my dear readers, while technology is a useful tool, it's also important to unplug and immerse yourself in the beauty of Iceland. Let the majestic glaciers, roaring waterfalls, and the ethereal Northern Lights captivate your senses. After all, the real essence of travel is to experience the world in its raw, unfiltered form.

Now, some of you might be thinking, "But what about the language barrier?" Well, let me assure you, most Icelanders speak English fluently. So, whether you're lost in translation or lost in the wild, help is just a phone call away.

Health and Safety

Medical Facilities: Iceland offers state-of-the-art medical facilities. Major towns have well-equipped hospitals, and Reykjavik, the capital, has several larger hospitals such as Landspítali (The National University Hospital of Iceland) located at Hringbraut, 101 Reykjavik. For minor ailments or non-emergency consultations, local health clinics, known as "Heilsugæsla," are accessible in almost every town.

Pharmacies: Pharmacies in Iceland are termed "Apótek" and are readily available in urban areas, offering a full range of medical supplies and prescription services. The major chains include Lyfja, which has numerous branches throughout the country, and Apótek, located centrally in larger towns and cities.

Vaccinations: No special vaccinations are required for Iceland beyond what is routinely given in your home country. However, it's recommended to have current protection against tetanus, measles, and other routine pathogens. Always consult with a travel health professional before departing.

Local Laws and Customs

Alcohol and Smoking: The legal drinking age is 20. Alcohol can be bought at Vínbúðin outlets, the state-run liquor stores, and at licensed restaurants and bars but not in supermarkets, except for low-alcohol beer. Smoking is prohibited in all indoor public places, public transport, and in restaurants and bars. Smoking near public buildings and entrances is also frowned upon.

Dress Code: There's no strict dress code, but practicality is vital. Weather can change drastically, so layered clothing, waterproof and windproof jackets, and good footwear are essential. Reflective gear is also recommended for pedestrians and cyclists during dark hours (which can be most of the day during winter).

Driving: Speed limits are strictly enforced, with gravel roads having a limit of 80 km/h and paved highways 90 km/h. Use headlights at all times, and note that off-road driving is illegal due to the potential damage to fragile vegetation.

Currency and Banking

Currency Exchange: The Icelandic Króna (ISK) can be exchanged at Keflavík Airport, banks across the country, and at many hotels. However, rates at the airport and hotels can be less favorable than banks in larger towns.

ATMs: These are widespread and accept international Visa and MasterCard, among others. They are reliable sources for cash, which is sometimes needed for smaller shops or rural areas, although card acceptance is very high.

Banking Hours: Most banks in Iceland operate from Monday to Friday, from 09:00 AM to 04:00 PM. Some bank branches in shopping malls may offer extended hours.

Electrical Standards

Voltage and Plug Type: The standard voltage is 230 V with a frequency of 50 Hz. Iceland uses type F power sockets, which are two-pin plugs similar to those used throughout continental Europe. Travelers from the UK, US, Canada, and Australia will need a plug adapter and possibly a voltage converter for devices operating at a different voltage.

Communication

Postal Services: Iceland's postal service is reliable and efficient, with services including letter and parcel delivery, both domestic and international. Main post offices are found in larger towns, and many are open during regular shopping hours, which can include weekends in urban areas.

Telephone: Public payphones are nearly obsolete due to widespread mobile coverage. To avoid high roaming fees, consider purchasing a local SIM card for your mobile device, which is available at the airport and many convenience stores.

Internet: Internet speeds in Iceland are among the highest globally, ensuring easy access for travelers to stay connected. Free Wi-Fi is commonly offered in accommodations, cafes, and public places like libraries and museums.

Local Transportation

Buses: The bus system in Iceland is robust in urban areas with less frequency in rural parts. Reykjavik's main bus company, Strætó bs, offers extensive routes throughout the capital and to major towns.

Car Rentals: Available at the airport and major towns. When renting, check terms especially regarding insurance policies covering gravel damage, which is common on Icelandic roads.

Taxis: Readily available in cities and at airports. They operate on a metered system, and it is customary to round up the fare for convenience.

Tourist Information

Tourist Offices: These can be invaluable for newcomers to Iceland, providing maps, tour bookings, and advice. The main tourist office in Reykjavik is located at Aðalstræti 2.

Guided Tours: Opting for guided tours, especially for activities such as glacier hiking, whale watching, or exploring volcanic caves, is advisable. This ensures safety through experienced guides who provide necessary equipment and expertise.

Cultural Etiquette

Greetings: While Icelanders are informal, they appreciate politeness. A firm handshake is standard when meeting someone for the first time. It's common to address people by their first name.

Conservation: Environmental preservation is taken very seriously. Stay on marked paths, don't disturb wildlife, and adhere to no-trace principles in natural areas.

Chapter 11

Cultural Insights

HISTORY OF ICELAND

In the realm of ice and fire, where the ground belches steam and the skies play host to kaleidoscopic light shows, there lies a land of many tales. This is Iceland, my dear readers, a place where the elements are as dramatic as the history.

It all started in the 9th century with the Norwegians, who, if I may be so bold, were the original hipsters. They were off to Iceland before it was cool. Literally. They braved the icy seas and the unforgiving climate and said, "This looks like a good place for a home." And so, they settled, bringing with them their livestock, their pagan gods, and a penchant for storytelling that still thrives today.

But let's not forget about the Vikings. Those bearded, horn-helmeted fellows with a passion for exploration and, occasionally, a bit of plundering. They too, found their way to this icy paradise and made it their own. Their sagas, filled with tales of heroic feats and epic battles, are as much a part of Iceland's history as the geysers and glaciers.

But alas, life in Iceland wasn't all about feasting on fermented shark and bathing in hot springs. The 13th century brought with it internal strife and civil war, followed by centuries of foreign rule. First, the Norwegians came back for a visit, then the Danes decided to drop by and, well, they never really left.

The foreign rule was no picnic, I assure you. Between the harsh winters, volcanic eruptions, and the plague, the Icelanders had their hands full. But, as they say, what doesn't freeze you solid or bury you in molten lava, makes you stronger.

Then, in the 19th century, the winds of change started to blow. A wave of nationalism swept over the country, and the Icelanders decided they'd had enough of being someone else's backyard. They started agitating for independence, and in 1944, after a vote that would make even the most apathetic of politicians break into a cold sweat, Iceland became an independent republic.

Nowadays, this land of fire and ice is known for its unique culture, breathtaking landscapes, and a language that can tie your tongue into knots. It's a place where you can soak in a geothermal pool while watching the Northern Lights dance across the sky, or take a stroll through a field of lava, if that's your cup of tea.

Art And Music

Now, if you've ever met an Icelander, you'll know they have a peculiar affinity for the arts. It's as natural to them as breathing the crisp Arctic air or eating fermented shark. In this land of fire and ice, creativity seems to bubble up from the volcanic soil, spilling over into every facet of life, but especially into art and music.

Let's start with the music. You may have heard of Björk or Sigur Rós, but this tiny island nation has a music scene as diverse and intense as its geothermal hot springs. From the heart-throbbing beats of techno festivals in Reykjavík to the soulful folk tunes echoing in the fjords, music is a language every Icelander speaks fluently.

Festivals are as common as puffins in summer, and just as colorful. Iceland Airwaves in November will have you tapping your toes to the rhythm of the Northern Lights. And Secret Solstice in June celebrates the midnight sun with a lineup as bright and endless as the daylight itself.

Iceland's art scene, on the other hand, is as unpredictable and intriguing as its weather. You'll find sculptures made from lava rock, paintings inspired by ancient sagas, and installations as avant-garde as they come. The Reykjavík Art Museum, for example, is a treasure trove of modern and contemporary art, housed in three distinct buildings throughout the city.

Street art is another phenomenon not to be missed. Reykjavík's grey concrete walls are transformed into vibrant murals, telling tales of trolls, elves, and the everyday life of Icelanders. It's as if the city itself is a canvas, and the artists are its storytellers.

Now, you might be wondering about traditional Icelandic art. Well, it's as unique as the language they speak. You'll find intricate wood carvings, delicate lacework, and hand-knitted woolen goods. The Lopapeysa, a traditional Icelandic sweater with a distinctive patterned yoke, is as much a work of art as it is a practical garment for the harsh Nordic winters.

And then there's the art of storytelling. With a literary tradition dating back to the Viking Age, Iceland is a nation of bookworms and poets. Every Icelander, it seems, has a story to tell. And they do so in a way that's as enchanting and captivating as their landscape.

Literature And Folklore

Icelandic literature, much like its weather, is a tempestuous blend of the quiet and the dramatic, the humorous and the tragic. It's a veritable smorgasbord of emotions and experiences, served up with a generous dollop of Icelandic wit and wisdom.

The sagas, for instance, are the country's literary pièce de résistance. Penned in the Middle Ages, they are stories of love, betrayal, heroism, and a fair bit of skulduggery. They chronicle the lives and trials of the early Viking settlers, painting a vivid picture of what life was like in those times. Not to mention, they are also a great source of amusement, with their tales of feuds, pranks, and often absurdly over-the-top heroics.

In the realm of modern literature, Iceland continues to punch above its weight, producing a disproportionate number of acclaimed authors for such a small population. Names like Halldór Laxness, the country's only Nobel laureate in literature, and Arnaldur Indriðason, a master of the Nordic noir genre, are just the tip of the iceberg. Their works, deeply rooted in the Icelandic landscape and psyche, offer a tantalizing taste of the country's unique cultural flavor.

But let's not forget the folk tales, those delightful yarns spun by the fireside to while away the long winter nights. Ghosts, trolls, elves, and other supernatural beings are the stars of these stories, reflecting the Icelandic people's deep-seated belief in the hidden world. It's a belief that's still alive today, with many a construction project rerouted to avoid disturbing an elfin rock or a troll mound.

And then there's the humor, as dry as the volcanic rock that dots the landscape. It's a humor born out of hardship and the sheer absurdity of living in such an inhospitable land. It's self-deprecating, often dark, but always with a twinkle in the eye. It's the humor of a people who've learned to laugh in the face of adversity, to find joy in the smallest things, and to make the best of whatever life throws at them.

To truly get under the skin of Iceland, one must dive headfirst into its literature and folklore. It's there that you'll find the soul of the country, in the sagas and the folk tales, the novels and the jokes. It's there that you'll understand why Icelanders are the way they are: resilient, good-humored, and with a touch of the fantastical in their worldview.

So, while you're munching on your hákarl or sipping your brennivín, why not pick up a book by an Icelandic author, or listen to a folk tale or two? It might just add an extra layer of enjoyment to your Icelandic culinary adventures. After all, there's nothing like a good story to aid digestion.

Cultural Etiquette Revisited

In that land of fire and ice, where geysers erupt with more punctuality than the most disciplined clock, and glaciers, those ancient frozen titans, stand guard, there exists a culture as captivating as its landscape. Picture this: you, the intrepid traveler, keen on not only observing but also partaking in these cultural nuances. But worry not! The Icelandic people, as warm as their geothermal hot springs, are ever ready to guide the uninitiated.

First, the matter of greetings. In other places, you might offer a hearty hand-shake, a peck on the cheek, or perhaps even an awkward hug. But here in Iceland, a simple "Góðan dag" (Good day) will suffice. No need for grand theatrical gestures or flamboyant salutations. Just a straightforward acknowledgment of the other's existence, paired with a friendly smile, will do the trick.

Next, let's ponder the gastronomic delights or, as some might say, the pecu-liarities of Icelandic cuisine. They have a fondness for things pickled, preserved, and fermented, a habit born of necessity in the harsh Arctic winters. You might be offered hákarl, fermented shark that has a scent reminiscent of a potent cheese left to age in a gym locker. Or perhaps, a taste of súrir hrútspungar, pickled ram's testicles that, despite the initial shock, have a surprisingly mild flavor. Now, you may balk at these offerings, but remember, when in Rome - or in this case, Reyk-javik - do as the locals do. A polite refusal is acceptable, but an adventurous spirit might just find these dishes more palatable than expected.

Now, on to the matter of punctuality. In some parts of the world, being fash-ionably late is the norm. Here, however, the geyser's influence is evident. Icelanders value punctuality, a trait as reliable as the next spout from Strokkur. Arriving late, even by a few minutes, is considered disrespectful. So, keep an eye on the clock, or better yet, set it to geyser time!

And finally, let's discuss the Icelandic tradition of the communal hot tub. Much like the English pub or the Italian piazza, the hot tub is a social hub, a place for lively debates, gossip, and the exchange of news. But remember, cleanliness is paramount. Before entering the tub, a thorough shower is expected, and don't be shy about it. After all, we are all friends in the hot tub.

Cultural Insights

In this land where the northern lights dance across the sky, and the midnight sun turns night into day, respect for nature is ingrained in every Icelander. Leave no trace is not just a suggestion, but a way of life. So, tread lightly, speak softly and let the magic of Iceland seep into your soul.

Chapter 12
Icelandic Wildlife

WILDLIFE WATCHING TIPS

Now, I can't rightly tell you how to go about it without invoking a bit of caution first. You see, it's all well and good to admire from afar, but you wouldn't want to end up on the wrong side of a puffin with a pecking problem, now would you? So, here are a handful of tips to make your wildlife watching as pleasant as a warm bowl of Icelandic lamb soup on a winter's day.

For starters, you'll want to keep a respectful distance. These critters aren't your household pets, and they don't take too kindly to strangers invading their space. And I don't know about you, but I'd rather not incur the wrath of a disgruntled reindeer. So, do yourself a favor and keep a safe distance. You'll find that your camera's zoom function comes in handy here.

Second, be patient. Wildlife watching ain't no race, and the animals aren't on our schedule. They might be snoozing, or feeding, or just plain hiding. So, take a leaf out of the tortoise's book and take your time. You'll find that patience pays off when you finally spot that elusive Arctic fox or whale breaking the water's surface.

Now, you'll also want to keep your movements slow and steady. Quick, sudden movements can startle the wildlife and send them scampering off before you've had a chance to admire them. And if you're on a boat watching whales or puffins, sudden movements can rock the boat and give everyone a good soaking. That's a surefire way to make yourself unpopular with your fellow travelers, I can tell you.

And speaking of popularity, remember to respect the environment. Don't leave any litter behind, and don't go picking flowers or disturbing nests. We're guests in these animals' home, after all, and we ought to behave like it. That means leaving everything just as we found it, and not taking anything but photographs and memories.

Now, if you're lucky, you might get to see some truly splendid sights. A herd of reindeer grazing on a hillside, a seal basking on an iceberg, a flock of puffins squabbling over a fish. But remember, these moments are a privilege, not a right. We're visitors in their world, and we should treat them with the respect they deserve.

And if you don't see anything? Well, don't be disheartened. Just being out in the wild, breathing in the fresh air, feeling the crunch of snow under your boots, that's a reward in itself. And who knows, maybe the wildlife is watching you, wondering what strange creature has wandered into their midst.

Common Animals And Where To Find Them

Now, should you fancy yourself a bit of a naturalist, Iceland offers a menagerie of curious critters that are sure to delight, confound, and occasionally, frighten. So, let's set forth on this wildlife expedition, not with a rifle and pith helmet, but with a spirit of discovery and a well-worn travel guide.

First off, let's discuss the majestic Icelandic horse. This is no ordinary equine, mind you. Brought over by the Vikings in the 9th and 10th centuries, these hardy beasts are more like the family dog than a simple farm animal. Small in stature, but large in personality, you'll find them dotting the countryside, their manes flowing in the arctic wind. You might be tempted to call them ponies, but don't let an Icelander hear you say that. These are horses, my friend, and proud ones at that.

Now, if you're more of a birdwatcher, Iceland's your paradise. You can't throw a stone without hitting a puffin. Not that you should throw stones at puffins, mind you. They're delightful creatures, with their brightly colored beaks and propensity for clownish antics. You'll find them along the coast during the summer months, nesting in cliffs and generally making a spectacle of themselves.

Of course, we can't forget about the seals. If you're lucky, you might spot one lounging on a rocky outcrop or perhaps doing a bit of fishing. The common seal and the grey seal are the two species you're most likely to encounter. Just remember to keep your distance. They might look cute and cuddly, but they're wild animals, after all.

Speaking of wild animals, let's talk about the Arctic Fox. This sly little creature is the only native land mammal in Iceland. In the winter, its fur turns a brilliant white, providing perfect camouflage against the snow. In the summer, it adopts a more casual brown coat. They're elusive creatures, but with a bit of luck and some patience, you might catch a glimpse of one in the Westfjords.

And then there's the Icelandic sheep. Now, you might think, "What's so special about a sheep?" But these are no ordinary sheep, I assure you. They're double-coated, you see, which makes them perfectly suited to the harsh Icelandic climate. And they're everywhere! You'll see them up in the mountains, down in the valleys, even wandering through town like they own the place.

Lastly, there's the whale, the leviathan of the deep. Whale watching is a popular pastime in Iceland, and for good reason. There's nothing quite like the sight of a humpback whale breaching the surface, or the awe-inspiring spectacle of a pod of orcas on the hunt. Just remember to bring your binoculars and your sea legs.

Safety Around Wildlife

Well now, here's a topic that might ruffle your feathers a bit - the critters of Iceland. Yes, sir, Iceland is home to a menagerie of wildlife, some as harmless as a church mouse, others as cantankerous as a drunk sailor. Now, don't go getting your knickers in a twist. I'm here to guide you through the wilderness, as safe as a babe in its mother's arms.

First off, let's talk about the birds. No, not the kind that flutter around in your garden, chirping merrily. I'm talking about the puffins, majestic creatures with beaks as colorful as a circus clown's nose. They're a sight to behold, but remember, they're not your pets. They're wild birds, with beaks sharp enough to snip off a careless finger. So, keep your hands to yourself, and admire them from a distance. And whatever you do, don't try to feed them your sandwich. They're not partial to ham and cheese.

Next, we've got the seals. Now, they're as slippery as a politician's promise, but twice as cute. They've got eyes as big as saucers and whiskers that twitch like a cat's tail. But don't be fooled by their innocent looks. They're wild animals, with teeth as sharp as a butcher's knife. So, keep your distance, and never try to pet them. They're not as cuddly as they look.

Then we've got the reindeer. Yes, the same ones that pull Santa's sleigh. They're a sight to behold, with antlers as big as tree branches. But they're not as friendly as Rudolph. They're wild beasts, with hooves as hard as a blacksmith's anvil. So, keep your distance, and never try to ride them. They're not your personal taxi service.

Finally, let's talk about the whales. Now, they're as big as a house, but as gentle as a lamb. They're a marvel to watch, but remember, they're not your swimming buddies. They're wild mammals, with tails as powerful as a steam engine. So, keep your distance, and never try to hitch a ride. They're not your personal ferry service.

Now, I'm not trying to scare you off. Iceland is a beautiful country, with wildlife as diverse as a patchwork quilt. But it's important to remember that these critters are not your playthings. They're wild animals, with their own rules and habits. So, treat them with respect, and they'll treat you the same.

And remember, safety first. Don't go traipsing around the wilderness like a bull in a china shop. Be mindful of your surroundings, and keep a safe distance from the wildlife. And whatever you do, don't try to take a selfie with a puffin. They're not as photogenic as they look.

Conservation Efforts

Now, let's turn our attention to a matter of significant importance, namely, the conservation efforts underway in Iceland. It's a topic that may not tickle your funny bone like a good old-fashioned Icelandic joke, but it's as vital as the air we breathe, the water we drink, and the pickled herring we reluctantly consume at local festivals.

Iceland, with its breathtaking landscapes of glaciers, geysers, and volcanic fields, is a country that deeply respects and protects its natural environment. Icelanders have a long history of living in harmony with the land, a tradition that continues in modern conservation efforts. They've realized that their land is not just a frozen playground for tourists in snowmobiles, but a precious resource to be preserved and protected.

The government of Iceland has taken significant strides in environmental conservation. They've got more protected parks than a nervous squirrel has acorns. These include national parks such as Þingvellir, Vatnajökull, and Snæfellsjökull, which cover over 13% of the country's total land area. And let me tell you, that's a whole lot of unspoiled wilderness, my friends.

Iceland's commitment to conservation doesn't stop at the land. The surrounding oceans are also under careful watch. The country has implemented sustainable fishing practices to ensure that the fish populations don't go the way of the dodo or, heaven forbid, common sense in a politician.

Renewable energy is another feather in Iceland's environmentally friendly cap. This little island harnesses the power of its abundant geothermal and hydroelectric resources like a pro wrestler in a headlock. Nearly all of its electricity and heat are produced from these renewable sources, making Iceland a global leader in clean energy.

Now, you may be thinking, "That's all well and good, but what can I, an intrepid traveler with a penchant for pickled herring, do to support these conservation efforts?" Well, dear reader, I'm glad you asked.

Firstly, respect the land. Stick to marked trails when hiking, don't litter, and for the love of all things holy, don't carve your initials into a 500-year-old moss-covered lava rock. Believe it or not, the moss takes centuries to grow back.

Secondly, support local businesses. Buy authentic Icelandic wool sweaters instead of cheap knock-offs, dine at local restaurants, and choose tour operators that prioritize sustainability. Your wallet has more power than you think.

Lastly, educate yourself and others about the importance of conservation. Knowledge is like a good joke; it's better when shared.

Chapter 13
Icelandic Festivals and Events

FESTIVAL ETIQUETTE AND TIPS

Now, don't you go thinking that Iceland is all about glaciers, waterfalls, and puffins with an uncanny resemblance to tuxedo-clad gentlemen. No, sir! Iceland is also a land of rollicking festivals, where locals and tourists alike gather to celebrate everything from music to elves. Yes, you heard that right, elves. But more on that later!

Now, if you're planning on attending one of these Icelandic hootenannies, there are a few things you should know. First off, the Icelanders are a friendly bunch, but they do appreciate a bit of respect for their traditions. After all, you wouldn't want someone coming into your home and putting their feet up on your coffee table, now would you?

So, when you're at one of these shindigs, do as the Icelanders do. Join in the singing, dance like nobody's watching, and for goodness sake, try the fermented shark! It might smell like something that's been left in the sun too long, but it's a local delicacy and refusing it could be seen as quite the faux pas.

Now, on to the elves. You might think it's all a bit of fun and games, but to many Icelanders, the Hidden Folk are as real as you and me. So, if you find yourself at the Elf School in Reykjavik or the Elf Garden in Hafnarfjordur, remember to show a little respect for the little folk. You wouldn't want to upset them and have all your socks go missing now, would you?

And speaking of clothes, dressing appropriately is key. Icelandic weather can be unpredictable, to say the least. One moment you could be basking in the sun, the next you could be caught in a hailstorm. So, don't forget to pack layers. And by layers, I don't mean just a light jacket. I'm talking thermals, waterproofs, and woolly hats. Even in the height of summer.

Don't forget, Icelandic festivals are not just about having a good time. They are also about community and togetherness. So, make sure to lend a hand if you see someone in need. Whether it's helping to clean up after the event or assisting a fellow festival-goer who's had one too many shots of Brennivin, every little bit helps.

Finally, remember to enjoy yourself. Yes, there are rules and etiquette to follow, but these festivals are about celebration and joy. So, don't get so caught up in doing everything right that you forget to have fun. After all, you're in Iceland, the land of fire and ice, elves and trolls, and some of the most spectacular sights you'll ever see. So, let loose, enjoy the music, taste the food, meet the people, and create memories that will last a lifetime.

After all, as the Icelanders say, "Þetta reddast". It will all work out. Now, go forth, my intrepid explorer, and enjoy all the festivities that Iceland has to offer!

Annual Festivals

Icelandic Festivals and Events

If there's one thing Icelanders know how to do better than producing world-class musicians and churning out crime novels that'll chill your bones, it's throwing a party. And let me tell you, they don't just throw any party. They throw a party that would make the most stoic Viking raise his drinking horn in a hearty skál!

Now, when you're venturing into this land of fire and ice, you might be wondering how on earth you'd fit into these high-spirited celebrations. Well, dear traveler, fear not! For I am here to guide you through the annual festivities of this Nordic wonderland.

In the frosty heart of winter, when the sun is as elusive as a politician's promise, Icelanders celebrate Þorrablót. This mid-winter feast is a smorgasbord of traditional Icelandic fare that might make the uninitiated blanch. But don't you go turning up your nose just yet! You haven't lived until you've sampled fermented shark or sheep's head. Just remember, a true adventurer never shies away from a culinary challenge!

Next on our merry list is the Reykjavík Arts Festival. This isn't your typical wine-and-cheese gallery hopping. Oh no, this festival is a cultural bonanza that spills onto the streets, transforming the city into a living, breathing canvas. Painters, poets, musicians, and even puppeteers come together to showcase their talents. It's as if the entire city is dipped in a pot of creativity, and the result is nothing short of magical.

But wait, the party doesn't stop there. Summertime brings with it the Secret Solstice Festival. This music festival coincides with the summer solstice, and let me tell you, there's nothing quite like partying under the midnight sun. World-renowned artists and local talents alike belt out tunes that echo across the valleys. And the best part? The sun doesn't set for the entire festival. That's right, you can dance the night away under a sky that refuses to darken!

Now, if you're more of a literary soul, then the Reykjavík International Literary Festival should be on your must-visit list. Here, you'll rub shoulders with acclaimed authors and fellow bookworms. Discussions, readings, and interviews are interspersed with good old Icelandic hospitality. And who knows, you might just find your next favorite book here!

But the grand finale, the pièce de résistance of Icelandic festivals, is the New Year's Eve celebration. Imagine this: a sky ablaze with fireworks, bonfires lighting up the night, and the streets filled with people singing and dancing. It's as if the entire country is bidding farewell to the old year and welcoming the new one with open arms. It's a sight to behold, and one that'll make your heart swell with joy.

Music And Art Events

Well now, let's shift our focus from the scrumptious Icelandic delicacies to the rich tapestry of music and art events that this chilly island has to offer. After all, what's a journey without a tune to tap your feet to or an art piece to marvel at? And let me tell you, when it comes to music and art, Iceland is no slouch. In fact, it's quite the opposite.

The Icelanders, bless their hearts, have an uncanny knack for turning the harsh, biting cold into a warm, inviting symphony of creativity. Now, you might think it's the hot geysers or the never-ending daylight in the summers that's got them all inspired. But, I reckon it's the sheer isolation of the place that's been the muse for these folks. There's something about being all alone in the middle of nowhere that gets the creative juices flowing.

Now, if you're a music enthusiast, you're in for a treat. Iceland is home to some of the most unique music festivals you'll ever come across. There's the Dark Music Days in Reykjavik, held during the darkest period of the year. The music is as somber as the name suggests, but there's a strange beauty to it that you won't find anywhere else.

Then, there's the Secret Solstice Festival, held during the summer solstice, where the sun doesn't set for three whole days. Imagine partying under the midnight sun, with music that ranges from folk to electronic, and artists from all over the world. It's a surreal experience that's worth every penny.

But music isn't the only thing that gets the Icelanders' creative gears turning. The country is also known for its vibrant art scene. Reykjavik, the capital city, is chock-full of art galleries and museums. The Reykjavik Art Museum, the National Gallery of Iceland, and the Einar Jónsson Museum are just a few of the places where you can admire the works of both local and international artists.

If you're more into street art, then you'll love the colorful murals that adorn the walls of Reykjavik. These aren't your run-of-the-mill graffiti, mind you. They're intricate pieces of art that tell stories of the city and its people. Each mural is unique, and you could spend hours just walking around, taking in all the beauty.

And let's not forget about the art festivals. There's the Reykjavik Arts Festival, which is an annual event that showcases a wide range of art forms, from visual arts to theater, dance, and music. Then, there's the Sequences Real-Time Art Festival, which focuses on time-based media, like video and performance art.

Local Celebrations

Iceland, dear reader, is a land of fire and ice, in so much as it is both very cold and has a lot of volcanoes. But it's also a land of celebration and merriment, and not just when the geysers aren't erupting. Now, it's time we talk about local celebrations, for they reveal the heart of a culture, and Iceland's heart is as warm as its hot springs.

One thing you'll quickly learn about Icelanders is that they love a good party. And why shouldn't they? Life on a volcanic island in the middle of the North Atlantic provides enough daily excitement to warrant a little jubilation. But the Icelandic people take their festivities to new heights, much like the geysers that punctuate their landscape.

The first celebration on our itinerary is Þorrablót, a mid-winter feast that makes Christmas dinner look like a light snack. Here, friends and family gather to devour traditional Icelandic dishes, some of which might test the fortitude of less adventurous eaters. The menu often includes fermented shark, smoked lamb, and boiled sheep's head. But fear not, dear traveler, for there's also plenty of Brennivín - a potent schnapps affectionately known as 'Black Death' - to help you swallow your fears, and your dinner.

Next up is the Summer Solstice, a time when the sun barely sets and the whole country becomes one big, round-the-clock party. It's a magical time, filled with music, dancing, and a sense of joy that can only come from 24 hours of daylight. The Secret Solstice Festival in Reykjavik is a particular highlight, featuring a line-up of international and local bands that will keep you dancing until the sun goes down... or rather, dips slightly below the horizon.

In the autumn, the Iceland Airwaves music festival takes center stage. Held in Reykjavik, this celebration of music and culture showcases the very best of Icelandic talent, alongside international acts. It's the perfect opportunity to immerse yourself in the local music scene, which is as diverse and vibrant as the country's landscape.

But of all the celebrations in Iceland, perhaps none is more anticipated than New Year's Eve, or as the locals call it, 'Gamlársdagur'. The evening begins with a family meal, followed by a bonfire, or 'brenna', where friends and neighbors gather to say goodbye to the old year. Then, as midnight approaches, the sky becomes a canvas of color as fireworks explode in a dazzling display of light and sound. The spectacle is so grand, it could almost make you forget the winter chill.

So, dear reader, if you find yourself in Iceland during one of these celebrations, do not hesitate to join in the festivities. Just be prepared for a lot of fun, a little bit of madness, and a whole lot of Brennivín. But remember, no matter how much you enjoy the fermented shark or the endless daylight, the true charm of these celebrations lies in the warmth of the Icelandic people.

Chapter 14
Icelandic Nightlife and Entertainment

NIGHTLIFE IN REYKJAVÍK

If you're of the mind to think that the midnight sun of Iceland's capital, Reykjavík, might tame the nocturnal activities of its citizens, then I've got a bridge in Brooklyn I'd like to sell you. Once the sun kisses the horizon and the clock strikes a late hour, the city bursts into a spectacle of merriment and mirth that would make a Mardi Gras parade blush.

The Reykjavík nightlife scene is as unpredictable as a cat on a hot tin roof. One moment you might be sipping a locally brewed stout in a quiet pub, and the next you could be dancing to the beats of an internationally acclaimed DJ in a packed nightclub.

Let's take, for instance, Kaffibarinn, a joint so popular, it's become something of a landmark. Its red London-style telephone box outside is as iconic as the Eiffel Tower to the Parisians. Once inside, you're greeted with an ambiance that's a delightful mix of a grandmother's living room and a trendy hipster hangout. The music is as varied as the patrons, and the cocktails are as potent as a preacher's sermon.

Now, if you're more inclined towards the beats that make your heart thump in rhythm, then Hurra is where you should be headed. Every night is a celebration here, with local bands, international DJs, and even the occasional poetry reading. The place has the energy of a thousand suns, and the music is as infectious as a yawn in a boring lecture.

For those who have a penchant for the theatrical, the cabaret scene at

Gaukurinn is not to be missed. The shows here are as flamboyant as a peacock in mating season, offering a delightful blend of drag, burlesque, and everything in between. It's an explosion of colors, sounds, and emotions that would make even the most stoic of Vikings smile.

And if you're looking for a bit of sophistication and culture, the Harpa Concert Hall is the place to be. The building itself is a work of art, shimmering in the night like a jewel on the city's skyline. Inside, you can enjoy performances ranging from classical orchestras to contemporary dance, all in an ambiance that's as elegant as a swan on a tranquil lake.

Of course, no night in Reykjavík would be complete without a visit to a late-night hot dog stand. The locals swear by them, and after a night of revelry, they're as comforting as a mother's embrace. The hot dogs are as juicy as a summer peach, and with a generous topping of fried onions, they're a culinary masterpiece that would make even a French chef nod in approval.

So, dear reader, if you're planning a visit to Reykjavík, do pack your dancing shoes and your party spirit. The city's nightlife is a delightful mix of the unexpected, the extraordinary, and the downright fun. It's a merry-go-round of entertainment that keeps spinning until the break of dawn, and sometimes even beyond. And remember, in the words of the locals, "Þetta reddast," which loosely translates to "everything will work out in the end." In Reykjavík, it always does, especially after dark.

Traditional Icelandic Entertainment

Well now, let's mosey on over to an aspect of Iceland that's sure to tickle your fancy - their traditional entertainment, which, trust me, is as rich and diverse as the country's stunning landscapes. I reckon it's about high time we shed some light on the merry activities of these hardy folks up North.

Now, you might imagine Icelanders to be a stern and serious bunch, what with their Viking heritage and all. But let me tell you, friend, they're as fond of a good laugh as the next man. The local comedy scene is a hoot and a half, with stand-up shows often held in Reykjavik's various pubs and theaters. They've got a humor that's as dry as a desert and as sharp as a tack, and it's sure to leave you rolling in the aisles.

But it's not all jests and japes up here. No sir, Icelanders are a musical bunch too, and they've got a tradition of singing that stretches back centuries. You haven't truly experienced the Icelandic spirit until you've huddled together with the locals in a cozy bar, singing traditional folk songs. They're sung in Icelandic, of course, but don't let that deter you - just open your mouth and let the spirit of the song carry you along.

Speaking of music, you can't talk about Icelandic entertainment without mentioning their music festivals. They've got a whole heap of them, from the Secret Solstice Festival, which celebrates the summer solstice with a round-the-clock music fest, to the Dark Music Days, a winter festival featuring contemporary and new music. These events are a testament to the Icelandic spirit - whether it's the brightest day or the darkest night, there's always a reason to celebrate.

Now, if you're the kind of person who enjoys a good story, you're in luck. Icelanders are renowned for their love of literature, and their storytelling traditions are as old as the country itself. Many an evening can be spent, nestled in a warm pub, listening to tales of trolls, elves, and hidden people. And if you're lucky, you might just spot one of these mythical creatures yourself!

Then there's the rímur, a form of epic poetry that dates back to the 14th century. Listening to a rímur performance is like stepping back in time, and it's a tradition that's still very much alive today. Even if you don't understand the words, the rhythmic cadence and the passion of the performers are sure to leave you mesmerized.

And let's not forget the national sport of Iceland - handball. If you've never seen a handball match before, you're in for a treat. It's a fast-paced, high-energy game that's sure to get your pulse racing. Whether you're cheering from the side-lines or joining in the action yourself, it's an experience you won't soon forget.

Cinema And Theatre In Iceland

Now, let's divert our attention to a different flavor of Icelandic culture, one that involves not just the palate but also the eyes and the ears - the grandeur of Icelandic cinema and theatre. Quite the spectacle, I assure you, and one that you shouldn't miss, lest you be considered a half-hearted tourist.

In this land of ice and fire, you might be surprised to find a rich tapestry of cinematic and theatrical arts. You see, Icelanders have a knack for storytelling. Maybe it's the long, dark winters that fuel their creative fires, or perhaps it's the mystique of the Northern Lights that sparks their imagination. Who knows? But one thing is certain - they sure know how to put on a show.

Now, the Icelandic cinema is a curious creature. It is as unpredictable as the geysers, as dramatic as their waterfalls, and as poignant as their midnight sun. It is a mirror reflecting the stark landscapes, the resilient spirit, and the subtle humor of the Icelandic people. Some films are as chilling as their glaciers, while others are as warm and comforting as their geothermal pools. You might find yourself laughing one moment, then shedding a tear the next. Such is the magic of Icelandic cinema.

Start your cinematic journey with a visit to the local movie house. Don't be surprised if you find yourself in a small, cozy room with just a handful of seats. Here in Iceland, cinema is an intimate experience, shared with a select few. But don't let the size fool you. These small cinemas pack a punch, showcasing a variety of films from local and international filmmakers. And don't worry about the language barrier. The Icelanders are considerate folks. They provide subtitles in English and sometimes, if you're lucky, in other languages too.

Now, if cinema is the heart of Icelandic culture, then theatre is its soul. The theatrical scene in Iceland is as vibrant and diverse as their flora and fauna. From classical plays to modern dramas, from musicals to comedy shows, there's something for every theatre enthusiast. The Harpa Concert Hall and Conference Center in Reykjavik is a must-visit. This architectural marvel is not just a feast for the eyes, but also for the ears and the heart. It is home to the Icelandic Symphony Orchestra and the Icelandic Opera, two of the country's finest performing arts groups.

Theatre in Iceland is a communal experience. It brings people together, much like their public swimming pools or their traditional feasts. It's not uncommon to see families, friends, and even complete strangers gathered together, engrossed in a play or a musical. And much like their cinema, Icelandic theatre is a reflection of their society - its joys, its sorrows, its triumphs, and its struggles.

Etiquette And Tips For Nightlife

As the sun descends and the moon takes the helm, Iceland, that frosty utopia in the North, takes on a whole new persona. The land of fire and ice, it seems, is also a land of revelry and delight when the stars come out to play. Now, as I am a man of considerable experience in the art of socializing, I thought it prudent to share some nuggets of wisdom on the subject of Icelandic nightlife.

Firstly, the Icelandic people are an amiable lot, so long as you don't mistake their stoicism for indifference. They are just as likely to engage in lively conversation as they are to quietly appreciate the beauty of their surroundings. If you find yourself in the company of locals, do not be afraid to engage them in conversation. They are a well-travelled and knowledgeable people, and you might just learn something new.

However, you must remember to mind your manners. The Icelanders are not fond of loud, disruptive tourists. It is best to speak softly and carry a big smile. And while we're on the subject of smiles, do remember that a genuine grin is always more appreciated than a forced one. The Icelanders can sniff out insincerity like a shark smells blood. Be authentic, and you will be welcomed.

When it comes to tipping, the Icelanders have a unique approach. They don't do it. Yes, you heard me correctly. In Iceland, service charges are included in the bill. Leaving extra money is not expected and can even be considered a tad bit awkward. So, save your coins for another round of that delicious Icelandic beer.

Now, let's talk about the actual nightlife. Iceland, despite its chilly demeanor, has a surprisingly vibrant club scene. Reykjavik, the capital city, is home to numerous bars and nightclubs where you can dance the night away to the rhythm of the aurora borealis. But beware, the nightlife here doesn't really kick off until around midnight, so don't show up at nine expecting a party.

Drinking in Iceland is a cherished pastime, but it can be as expensive as a new pair of good boots. The price of alcohol is steep due to the heavy taxes imposed on it. However, there are ways around this. Many locals pre-drink at home before heading out to the clubs. So, if you're invited for some pre-club festivities, consider it a blessing.

Dress code, you ask? Well, the Icelanders are a practical bunch. With the weather being as unpredictable as a cat on a hot tin roof, it's best to dress in layers. A nice shirt or blouse coupled with a warm sweater should do the trick. And remember, comfort trumps style in the land of fire and ice.

Lastly, if you find yourself a little too tipsy to find your way back to your hostel, fear not. The locals are always willing to help a lost soul. Just remember to ask politely and thank them profusely. After all, good manners are a universal currency.

Conclusion

As we turn the last page of the "Iceland Travel Guide 2024," we're just getting started. Katrín Frost has shown us the best spots, from hot water pools to tall, snowy mountains, with clear and simple tips. We've learned about where to stay, what foods to try, and how to be safe and kind to nature.

Think of this book like a friendly chat with a guide who knows Iceland's secrets. It's full of good ideas for your trip, but remember, things change, so keep asking around and looking up the latest info to make your trip even better.

We hope this book makes you excited to pack your bags and head to Iceland, ready for a great adventure. Imagine the stories you'll tell about the Northern Lights or the cool festivals you'll see. Keep this book close as you step into Iceland's amazing world, and go make some unforgettable memories.

Happy travels, and enjoy every moment in the beautiful land of Iceland!

Step-by-Step Action Plan After Reading the Guide:

1 Detailed Research:

• Deepen your understanding of the areas that intrigue you. Websites like Visit Iceland and Guide to Iceland are treasure troves for up-to-date details.

• Watch travel vlogs focused on Iceland to visualize your journey and get personal tips from those who've tread the path before you.

2 Community Engagement:

• Find and join Iceland travel communities on platforms like Reddit or Facebook to ask questions, read about recent traveler experiences, and even find travel buddies.

- Use platforms like Meetup to find local events or gatherings that might coincide with your visit.

3 Reservations and Bookings:
- Start by booking your flights, then secure accommodations, especially if you're traveling during peak seasons.
- For activities that require reservations, such as the Blue Lagoon or popular guided tours, book these well in advance.

4 Packing Strategically:
- Create a packing list tailored to your activities—include layers for changing weather, sturdy hiking boots, a swimsuit for hot springs, and adapters for charging devices.
- Don't forget to pack essentials like a first-aid kit, travel-sized toiletries, and any specific gear you might need for photography or other hobbies.

5 Language Prep:
- Invest time in learning Icelandic phrases through apps like Duolingo, or pick up a pocket-sized Icelandic phrasebook.
- Practice key phrases such as greetings, directions, and dining requests to show locals your effort to embrace their language.

6 Tech Toolkit:
- Download offline maps through apps like Google Maps or MAPS.ME.
- Consider apps for real-time weather updates in Iceland, such as Veður or the Icelandic Met Office's app, and familiarize yourself with them.

7 Safety Measures:
- Keep a list of emergency contacts, including the local emergency number (112), embassy information, and contacts for your accommodations.
- Review your health insurance policy and consider additional travel insurance that covers medical emergencies and trip cancellations.

8 Checklists:
- Run through a pre-travel checklist a week before departure. This should include tasks like notifying your bank of travel plans, confirming reservations, and double-checking flight times.
- Prepare your home for your absence by securing windows and doors, pausing mail delivery, and perhaps arranging for a friend or neighbor to check in periodically.

9 Embrace Flexibility:
- While a detailed itinerary is great, Iceland's weather can be unpredictable. Be prepared to swap days around or substitute activities based on the day's conditions.
- Have a backup plan for indoor activities like museums or local cultural centers in case of inclement weather.

Conclusion

10 Leave Gaps for Discovery:

• Plan free days or afternoons in your itinerary for spontaneous exploration—this could mean wandering Reykjavik's streets, finding a local café, or taking a surprise detour on a scenic drive.

Get Your Full-Color eBook & Maps!

Want to see Iceland in all its colorful glory? We've got you covered! Inside your "Iceland Travel Guide 2024," you'll find a handy QR code. Give it a quick scan with your smartphone or tablet, and voilà, you'll unlock some awesome digital extras:

1 The Full-Color eBook: Dive into the vivid, full-color pages in the eBook that bring to life the stunning landscapes of Iceland. From the deep blues of the Atlantic to the fiery reds of its volcanoes, get ready for an eye-popping preview of your trip.

2 Colorful Digital Maps: Get easy-to-use, colorful maps that you can zoom in on and explore. These will be super helpful when you're navigating Iceland's towns and wilds.

We know the book is handy, but sometimes you don't want to carry it everywhere. With these digital bonuses, you have the freedom to explore without extra weight. The images and maps in the paperback are in black and white and smaller, to keep things simple. But with your digital bonus, you can see all those places pop on your screen in big, bright colors.

So, keep your book safe at your hotel or cozy Airbnb and use the digital versions when you're out and about. Have all the info you need right in your pocket, and make your Iceland adventure as light and carefree as the island's breezy summers.